KATHERINE THOMSON is a multi-award winning playwright and screenwriter. Her television credits include *Mr & Mrs Murder*, *Australia on Trial*, *Darwin's Brave New World*, *Rogue Nation*, *Killing Time*, *East West 101*, *Satisfaction*, *BlackJack*, *Wildside*, *Grass Roots*, *Halifax f.p.* and she was the co-writer of the Australian and Canadian co-production *Answered by Fire* which received the Gold AWGIE in 2006. Katherine wrote the documentary *Unfolding Florence—the Many Lives of Florence Broadhurst* which was directed by Gillian Armstrong. It screened at Sundance Film Festival and won the AWGIE Award for Best Documentary and Best Television Script at the QLD Premier's Literary Awards in 2006.

Katherine's numerous and critically acclaimed theatre credits include *King Tide*, *Harbour*, *Diving for Pearls*, *Barmaids*, *Fragments of Hong Kong*, *Navigating*, *Kayak*, *Mavis Goes to Timor*, *Wonderlands and Darlinghurst Nights*. In 2006, Katherine was awarded the Australian National Playwrights Centre Award for her substantial contribution to the Australian theatre industry. In 2010 Katherine's play *King Tide* was adapted for ABC Radio Airplay. It won an AWGIE for Best Radio Adaptation. She is currently in development on numerous film and television projects including a feature documentary with director Gillian Armstrong about the acclaimed costume designer Orry Kelly, which is due for release in 2014.

Navigating

KATHERINE THOMSON

CURRENCY PRESS
SYDNEY

CURRENCY PLAYS

First published in 1998
by Currency Press Pty Ltd
PO Box 2287, Strawberry Hills, NSW, 2012, Australia
enquiries@currency.com.au
www.currency.com.au

Reprinted 2001, 2008, 2013

NATIONAL LIBRARY OF AUSTRALIA CIP DATA

Thomson, Katherine, 1955–
Navigating.
9780868195742 (paperback.)
1. Whistle blowing—Drama. I. Title
A822.3

Typeset by Stefania Cox for Currency Press.
Cover design by Katy Wall for Currency Press.
Cover photo shows Cecelia Ireland (left) and Noni Hazlehurst in the 1998 Sydney Theatre Company production (photo Tracey Schramm).

Currency Press acknowledges the Traditional Owners of the Country on which we live and work. We pay our respects to all Aboriginal and Torres Strait Islander Elders, past and present.

Australian Government

Publication of this title was assisted by the Commonwealth Government through the Australia Council, its arts funding and advisory body.

Contents

ACKNOWLEDGEMENTS

With thanks to Robyn Nevin, Roger Hodgeman, Richard Wherrett, Wayne Harrison and Marion Potts; the actors, sound designers and stage managers of both the QTC/MTC and the STC productions for their support in developing the text through the rehearsal periods. Grateful thanks too to the numerous colleagues whose generous feedback and support contributed to the development of the play, and, as always, to Paul Thompson.

In particular, I thank Whistleblowers Australia, and acknowledge the many whistleblowers across the country who shared their stories and their lives with me. Their generosity, courage, and trust has been an inspiration.

Katherine Thomson
September 1998

The Public and the Private

Brecht's *Fears and Miseries of the Third Reich* has been a major influence on my work as a teacher, director, writer and dramaturg. I have directed the play twice and frequently use scenes as examples in my playwriting classes. It was often in my mind as I worked with Katherine Thomson on her play *Navigating*.

Strictly speaking, *Fears and Miseries* is not really a single play but a cycle of 24 short plays varying in length from two to twenty minutes. The cycle charts the rise of Hitlerism in Germany from 1933–38 and is sometimes performed under the alternative title *The Private Life of the Master Race*. The plays were written in exile around 1938 and demonstrate Brecht's remarkable ability to read the complex social and political dynamics of his time. As one of the most gifted dramatists of the twentieth century, he chose to represent this world in short, carefully selected, realistic scenes where parents learn to fear their children, pupils tyrannise teachers, wives lose faith in their husbands and friends discover they no longer trust each other. Ordinary people are seen to be conducting ordinary private lives, but they are all influenced by public events as Nazism creeps under the doors and seeps through the walls contaminating every human exchange. At the same time, as we watch these characters we see that, through their sins of omission and sins of commission, with a few noble exceptions, they were sealing their own fate. At one point one character says, 'It's nothing to do with us, we're Protestants', at another point a husband bids farewell to his wife saying, 'It'll only be for a few weeks', as he hands her the fur coat he knows she will not need until winter. In the best traditions of political theatre, Brecht's intention was not only to render the world understandable, but also to suggest that it is changeable.

The ability to see the large public picture and to capture its essence in scenes of small private exchanges also characterises the work of Katherine Thomson. When we look at her recent trilogy of plays, *Diving for Pearls* (1991), *Barmaids* (1991) and *Navigating* (1998), we are struck by the author's ability to see the big picture and engage with the seemingly incomprehensible social forces that are shaping our world at the end of the twentieth century. Like it or not, in the market economy our lives are influenced by privatisation, globalisation, downsizing and outsourcing. Mesmerised by the nomadic and unpatriotic nature of capital, we live in a period when the people seem to be serving the economy, rather than the economy serving the people. This very strange world is reflected back to us in Katherine Thomson's plays where characters struggle to hold onto their jobs, their relationships and their lives, as everything around them changes in an unpredictable way, at an incomprehensible speed.

Navigating represents a significant progression in Katherine Thomson's work. Building upon her already established ability to locate three dimensional characters within socially specific landscapes, the play emphasises the element of historical time and the sense in which the past casts its shadow over the present. The play raises the moral questions of how we are as a nation and how we, as individuals, deal with history. The skeletons in the public closet make it difficult for us to conduct our lives. *Navigating* is very much about honesty and morality in a period where such ideas are, to say the least, problematic. At the end of the nineteenth century I fondly imagine that people had some kind of optimistic faith in religion, science or socialism, but now, as we prepare to enter the twenty-first century, it seems that many of our gods have forsaken us. The market determines our value and all we believe in is money. In the circumstances how do we tell right from wrong? This is the question posed by *Navigating*.

The ability to marry the public and the private is but one of the qualities I admire in Katherine Thomson's work. Another attraction is her unsentimental treatment of her characters coupled with her remarkable ear for dialogue. She has the quality that one looks for in a writer—a unique, authentic voice.

As a dramaturg I have now worked with Katherine on several occasions. Our working relationship is enhanced by a shared passion for politics and a shared sense of humour. Equally we benefit from having worked as actors. I believe it was George Bernard Shaw who once said something to the effect that the sole function of a dramatist was to provide the material for great performances by actors. Certainly it is no accident that so many playwrights were also actors—Shakespeare,

Molière and Pinter spring immediately to mind. When Katherine and I discuss a scene we are always mindful of how each moment might play, and although we never admit it, we are also imagining ourselves in each role.

In searching for a suitable analogy to describe our working relationship I am tempted to suggest a nautical equivalent such as captain and first mate. But as I don't know one end of a ship from another, it might be more appropriate to talk in terms of a champion boxer and his trainer. Brecht would certainly approve of this image— Muhamed Ali and Angelo Dundee locked in furious debate, nutting out a strategy between rounds. Attractive as this analogy might be, I would have to confess it wildly overstates the role of the dramaturg. In real life I am more of a back seat driver. I am quite capable of saying things like 'you're going a bit fast', 'slow down', 'you can go left here… whoops, sorry, one way'. As an experienced back seat driver I know that Katherine Thomson knows what she is doing. She knows where she's going. I hope I don't get on her nerves because one day I would like to hitch a ride with her again… cruising the public streets in her private car.

Paul Thompson
Associate Professor of Film and Television
New York University

Janet Andrewartha (seated) as Isola and Jackie Weaver as Bea in the 1997 Queensland Theatre Company/Melbourne Theatre Company production. (Photo: Melanie Gray)

Navigating was first produced by Queensland Theatre Company and Melbourne Theatre Company at Suncorp Theatre, Brisbane, on 11 October 1997, and Fairfax Theatre, Victorian Arts Centre, Melbourne, on 6 November 1997, with the following cast:

IAN	Robert Grubb
BEA	Jacki Weaver
ISOLA	Janet Andrewartha
BRENT	Roger Oakley
DARCY	Barbara Lowing
DIACK SHAW	Michael Forde
PAM SHAW	Claire Crowther

Director, Richard Wherrett
Designer, Michael Scott-Mitchell
Costume Designer, Dale Ferguson
Lighting Designer, David Whitworth
Music, Andy Arthurs
Dramaturgy, Paul Thompson & Richard Wherrett

Following the first production the script was substantially revised. The published text was first performed by Sydney Theatre Company at the Playhouse, Sydney Opera House, on 20 July 1998, with the following cast:

IAN	Graeme Blundell
BEA	Noni Hazlehurst
ISOLA	Rachel Szalay
BRENT	Francis Gleenslade
DARCY	Cecilia Ireland
DIACK SHAW	Peter Carroll
PAM SHAW	Judi Farr

Director, Marion Potts
Designer, Stephen Curtis
Lighting Designer, Nigel Levings
Music and Sound Designer, Andrée Greenwell
Dramaturgy, Paul Thompson & Richard Wherrett

CHARACTERS

BEA, about 49 years old. Even as a child, would have been described as 'capable', 'responsible'. Possibly 'plain'.

ISOLA,* ten years younger.

BRENT, late 30s, early 40s.

IAN DONNELLY, mid 40s. Clean, smooth (in that small-town sort of way).

PAM SHAW, old enough to have had a 35-year-old son.

DICK SHAW, same.

DARCY, younger than Bea and Isola. Normally practical. Down to earth.

*Use Italian pronunciation, i.e., short vowels, as in 'izzella'.

SETTING

Nothing needs to be literal. an occasional chair might be needed, something will need to function as a desk.

All locations can be achieved with lighting and props, although a clincer-boat at the end is desirable. One might see the corner of the figurehead that is stored in the boatshed.

A soundscape would assist the creation of location.

ACT ONE

Out of the darkness comes the sound of a piano being played with heavy hands. It is joined by twenty or so voices of a small-town, amateur choir doing their best with 'Va pen siero'.

One voice will begin to be heard above the others. It's BEA, *oblivious to the fact that her singing becomes louder with each breath she takes.* BEA *is in her late forties—an open soul, capable and trusting.*

Her sister, ISOLA, *is in another pool of light.* ISOLA *is ten years younger, more delicate in appearance. Withdrawn and vulnerable in demeanour. Her style of singing is much more reticent. She glances at* BEA, *reacting to her rather robust singing.*

Nearby, PAM SHAW, *a woman in her fifties, sings meekly, and in the men's section her husband,* DICK SHAW, *sings with determination.* BRENT, *a man awkward in his own body, fidgeting even as he sings, can't help but glance at* ISOLA. *Near him, wrapped up in his own voice, the confident, charming* IAN DONNELLY *is only too aware of how much the musical burden is falling on his shoulders.*

The singing ends, there's the sound of applause. They all nod little bows as they pick up their music, but IAN *steps forward, in a gesture that is unplanned.*

IAN: Thank you. That was the prisoner's chorus from *Nabucco*. In the capacity of secretary of the choir, on this glorious Sunday, I wonder if I might take the liberty of leading us in prayer.

> BEA *looks a little surprised, but bows her head with the rest of the choir.* IAN *is unused to praying, let alone leading the prayer.*

Dear Lord, we pray for guidance to the Minister of Justice, other Honourable Members of Parliament visiting our town this weekend, for the citizens of our Shire present here today. For their representatives—the councillors and members of Dunbar Development Group gathered here before you. We ask you to bless us with employment and growth as it pleaseth you, and as we know could be so enhanced from the proposed new prison in our Shire. We have been sorely hit by hard times of late, Oh Lord, but we know with your help we can flourish once again. We have lived, Oh Lord, with the old prison up on the hill for as long as most of us have been alive, and until it closes next year, a daily reminder of our own fortune, freedom and of the true path. We ask you to bless us, and the other shortlisted sites, we thank you for the opportunity to show the Honourable Members the site our Shire and... the facilities we offer. We ask your blessings too, Oh Lord, the representatives of Carter Corrections, American Detention Industries and Silver Security Systems who have travelled so widely to be with us today.

A few mumbles of 'Amen', but IAN *is inspired to continue.*

For we are a people who have always looked to the future, Lord, with your guidance in our enterprise... and faith. Amen.

Sound of 'Amen'. IAN *is, uncharacteristically given his usual confidence, deeply relieved.*

Thank you. And now Peter Greig, Chairman of Dunbar Development Group...

Sound of applause.

TRANSITION to a riverside patch of land, not far from the entrance bar. ISOLA *and* BEA *are waiting near a wheelbarrow on which is sitting a figurehead, covered with a canvas cloth.*

ISOLA *stares out to sea.* BEA *idly twirls a smooth old stick in her hand—a diviner's stick.* BEA *looks at her watch, then has a quiet laugh to herself.*

ISOLA: What?

BEA: Ian Donnelly praying. Ian Donnelly's no more religious than I am. I've heard the language at work, thank you. Once he started it was like he was tangled up in some dreadful web that was growing out of his mouth. I thought any minute now he's going to break into song and pull out his tambourine.

ISOLA: He had to pray. All the visiting politicians are in the Parliamentary Prayer Group.

BEA: How do you know that?

ISOLA: [*galvanised*] That's our phone.

BEA: Since when have you got ears like a bat?

ISOLA: Ssssh.

> *They both listen.*

BEA: We're not expecting a call.

ISOLA: It's stopped. Since when do you have to be expecting a call to get one?

> *Pause.*

BEA: Fancy this [*the stick*] still being tucked away in all that junk. In one piece. [*Carved:*] 'G.S.' Grandpa Samson. He was a dear old chap. Telling people where to sink their bores.

ISOLA: I don't remember.

BEA: Of course you don't. That's why I'm telling you. He'd say, 'You imagine the water up here, then you find it out there.' That he had to have the idea of the water, before he could find the water. I used to puzzle over that.

ISOLA: They're not coming. I told you.

BEA: Give them another few minutes.

ISOLA: They'll all have gone to the Business Club for lunch. What exactly did he say? Ian. Ian Donnelly.

BEA: I told you.

ISOLA: [*looking off*] Perhaps you weren't precise.

BEA: I said, 'What time will you be finished showing around the politicians and the prison company bigwigs?' and he said, 'About one o'clock', and I said, 'Well, when you have, bring some of the service club fellows down to the land next to our place because my sister and I have got something to show you. That we'd like to donate to the town. That we think would make a memorial.' Then he said, 'For what?' And I said, 'Well, what would do you think it's for, the Battle of Trafalgar? It's thirty-five years this year since the *Harmony* went down.' 'Oh,' he said. [*Pause*] How about that, that's what's odd. The wind's dropped, hasn't it? We can take the ballast out of our pockets. Don't slouch, Issie. Once you turn forty you'll be putting yourself in line for a great big hump. End up doubled-over like old Mrs Jenna sits outside the Council of a Tuesday. Sits on the seat for a view of the entrance, and what does she see but her own.

A beat, then ISOLA *laughs. Just a bit.*

That's more like it. [*Her smile fades*] Are you pre-menstrual, Issie?

ISOLA: No.

BEA: Well, you can't be, of course. Unless you and I are getting out of synch. Which I suppose won't be too far away. Dear, they were interested, the girls at work. [*As she recounted it and as she sits next to* ISOLA] When Issie and I were both in the city and I foisted myself onto her in Brink Street—fourteen years—

ISOLA: Fifteen—

BEA: We've always been within a day of each other starting. A model of co-ordination Babs called it. Bake-off day, last Friday. I'm in with that little group now, you can feel it. [*Pause*] They were saying how lucky we are. Aren't you lucky to be that close? To have each other. You and your sister. [*Pause*] You could pop in sometime, they think the world of you. They do.

ISOLA *doesn't respond.*

Is it a little bit of depression perhaps? What you're feeling.

ISOLA: No.

BEA: Like depression.

ISOLA: [*looking offstage*] Someone's coming.

BEA: It's who, is it… ? Brent come for lunch. Early. On his tod.

ISOLA: Say we have to go out.

BEA: He was pleased as punch, you can't do that to people. He's not still trying it on.

ISOLA: No.

BEA: I wouldn't want to think of him still having his hopes up.

ISOLA: Nothing to do with me.

BEA: I mean, you know he's harmless, I know he's harmless. Am I right to think he's harmless?

ISOLA *is silent.*

I take it that's a yes.

ISOLA *nods.*

Good. Well, let's face it, he's handy with that electric drill. He'd probably bore it through his head if you told him to. Here he is. [*Sotto*] We've asked him for today, but that can do him for a while.

[*To* BRENT] How are you, Mr Bailey Junior?

BRENT: Here I am—better stop talking about me. Blackberries are fierce. So this [*the figurehead*] is it, eh?

> BEA *pulls off the canvas.*

Well, she'll need some restoration. Weatherproofing. Put up on a plinth.

BEA: You don't think they might just want to stick her up the hill in the wheelbarrow? Having a loan? My thought is overlooking the bar, but Issie's the one with the eye.

ISOLA: You didn't pass Ian Donnelly, did you? On his way over here?

BRENT: No.

ISOLA: They're not coming. I knew they wouldn't. I'll go and heat up lunch.

BRENT: Good-oh.

ISOLA: Are you still allergic to mushrooms?

BRENT: Yes.

ISOLA: It's mushroom soup. You'll have to pick them out. Then we're having chicken and mushrooms. Followed by mushroom ice-cream.

> *Pause.*

BRENT: I can take a joke.

> ISOLA *starts to leave.*

BEA: Wait, Issie, please. [*To* BRENT] What about a photo then? To give them an idea. We've gone to all the trouble of lugging it over here.

BRENT: [*not wanting to be part of this at all*] The camera gear's in the car.

BEA: Quick sticks.

BRENT: [*to* ISOLA] Want to give me a hand?

ISOLA: No.

> BRENT *goes off in the direction of the house.*

For God's sake.

BEA: What?

ISOLA: He's humouring you. Can't you see that no one wants a monument?

BEA: I beg your pardon.

ISOLA: It's two generations ago. Everyone's forgotten.

From left: Graeme Blundell as Ian Donnelly, Francis Greenslade as Brent, Noni Hazlehurst as Bea and Judi Farr as Pam Shaw in the 1998 Sydney Theatre Company production. (Photo: Tracey Schramm)

BEA: Certainly that's the impression—

ISOLA: It's dragging attention to ourselves.

BEA: It's giving something to the town. Now that we're back in Dunbar, it'll show we want to be… part of the community.

ISOLA: As if we're trying to apologise.

BEA: You've been told a hundred times, our father didn't cause that boat to sink—

ISOLA: He was the skipper—

BEA: It was a freak wave. You know that. Don't go all topsy-turvy on me. Nightfall he was still out there in the blackness, diving under, searching for kiddies' bodies. They had to beg him to stop.

ISOLA: If it wasn't his fault—

BEA: A freak wave, by it's very nature…

ISOLA: —why do people avoid the subject?

BEA: I don't know.

ISOLA: Because they don't want to remember.

BEA: Because they don't know how. Because there should have been a memorial built the year it happened. Somewhere to reflect. For everyone who was affected, including us, I might add—

ISOLA: If people wanted a bloody memorial they'd have had a bloody memorial by now.

BEA: What in heaven's name's got into you? Thirty-five years ago this November, twenty-eight children drowned out there. And you can't tell me that where there's a tragedy of that calibre any other place'd have somewhere to mark it. The River Lethe, that teacher we had in form four once called it. He said it meant the river of forgetfulness. I've never forgotten that. He had brains. A real teacher. He used to say 'let us remember' on the anniversary, remember all the kiddies. And be extra nice to us. And to me. You wonder how much is still out there. Lodged in the bar. If they remember Singapore, we can remember that. Somewhere to come and think. If this private prison goes ahead there'll be newcomers galore. People will ask what's that monument for and—

ISOLA: I don't see why—

BEA: Something happened here once, it affected a lot of people, and the only interesting monument this town's got is the red brick toilet block smack bang in the middle of the main street because the city engineer before this one owed that Greek plumber a favour. We've discussed this, Issie, I don't know what's got into you.

> ISOLA *starts to leave but* DARCY *enters. She's a woman in her twenties. She would normally present as confident and self-assured, but currently she has the fragile air of someone needing to be alone. She is dressed in comparatively light clothes, and has an envelope in her hands. She can't quite look* BEA *in the eye.*

DARCY: Hi. I saw you through the trees.

BEA: Good morning.

DARCY: [*the figurehead*] Oh wow… Where's she from?

BEA: Someone gave it to our father once, we're not really sure. [*Prompting*] Isola. I think the young lady has something for you. [*To* DARCY] She'll give you a receipt later. Dear, you must be freezing. Better go and get yourself warmed up.

ISOLA: She's training herself not to feel the cold. For sailing round the world, right?

DARCY: [*to* BEA, *as she hands the envelope to her*] Actually it's for you. A woman was at the gate when I was coming in. [*To* ISOLA] One day, maybe.

BEA: [*looking at the envelope*] What woman?

DARCY: Short woman with dark curly hair.

BEA: Deb. [*To* ISOLA] She rang last week, said she wanted to send me something—

DARCY: She wouldn't say her name.

BEA: [*to* ISOLA] I don't know what the mystery is. Wanted to know if I still worked for Council…

DARCY: She did want to bring it to you herself but her family was waiting. In the car. So I promised to put it in your hand. And to make sure you know they're moving up north tomorrow. For good, she said. You'd know what to do.

> BEA *doesn't open the envelope.* DARCY *is fascinated by the figurehead.*

The one on the *Cutty Sark*'s like this. [*She stretches out an arm*] She's got long strands of horse's hair all caught up in her fingers. This one's beautiful, too.

ISOLA: We made a bit of a mess clearing junk out of the boatshed to get her… Sorry.

BEA: [*to* ISOLA] We'll put it all back. [*To* DARCY] Thank you.

DARCY: Hope it's not bad news.

> BEA *doesn't answer.* DARCY *gets the hint and goes.*

BEA: Hope it's not bad news. She puts a shiver down my spine, that girl. Talk about a long face, not to mention never looks a person in the eye. What's her name?

ISOLA: It's a funny name…

BEA: I thought you got all that written down. Find it out. 'I'll be coming and going. I'll be using it as a retreat.' There's some sort of secret there. On the dole, of course, that's written all over her. All the time in the world.

ISOLA: She said she dreamed one night of a boatshed, then the next day she found it. What's in the envelope?

BEA: [*still looking in* DARCY*'s direction*] De facto in the clink, I'll bet. One night we'll wake up to the escapee Craig in the garden and have the S.A.S. jumping out of the helicopters onto the shrubs. Still waters.

> BEA *opens the envelope and begins to read. There are a number of pages to this letter, including copies of bank statements.* BRENT *returns puffing, lugging his camera bag.*

BRENT: She your new tenant?

> BEA *doesn't respond. She's head-down reading the letter.*

Just saw all the black cars sail past—Peter Greig in the back seat with the Minister for Justice, chin held up and his chest puffed out. Between us, that I said that. Off the record, as we say. Word is the companies like the proposed site. Real prison terrain apparently. But I suppose they'd say that whichever town they're in.

BEA: [*pre-occupied with the contents of the letter*] Brent—we might need to make lunch next week.

BRENT: Oh.

ISOLA: What if they come?

BEA: They can come to the house.

ISOLA: See you.

BRENT: Issie. How about a snap? Your hair looks lovely done like that.

> ISOLA *goes.*

Well. A man can't take a trick.

BEA: Brent. Issie and I are like a pair of pockets. We wouldn't have it any other way. Not many people know this, but when we were in the city, when our Aunt Sissy who minded us died, I went to court for Issie. She wasn't even in high school. I'd just turned twenty-one. Foster her out, they tried to tell me. So you'll understand if I'm on the protective side…

> *Carefully,* BEA *folds up the letter.*

BRENT: That bad news you've got?

BEA: I'm not sure.

BRENT: Or a love letter? You can tell me.

BEA: Could I leave this [*the figurehead*] to you to get back into the boatshed?

BRENT: Downhill all the way.

BEA: [*the photos*] From a couple of different angles perhaps. Give them the general idea.

BRENT: Sure. [*The figurehead*] Once her lips and eyes are painted up, bit of shading in the cleavage, that's a lady's tip I read somewhere. [*Pause*] I don't mean anything. With Isola and me.

> *He starts setting his camera.* BEA *starts to leave. She hesitates.*

BEA: You're a good person, Brent. I just think a bloke might be happier if he didn't even try.

TRANSITION. Lights change to early evening. Sound of wind, and wood creaking.

IAN, *in his office, pulls a long-armed extension mirror from its support, shakes a bottle of hair dye and skims quickly over the instructions.*

IAN: [*muttering, reading*] 'Upward sweeping motion… avoid eyes… scalp… not suitable for… '

> *Can't be bothered reading the fine print, he takes the lid off.* BEA *appears in the doorway behind him. He doesn't see her. She can't believe her eyes, tries to sneak out, but—*

Jesus Christ. Yes?

BEA: I didn't know you died your hair.

IAN: I don't.

BEA: I won't tell a soul. It won't go any further than the finance section. Seriously, Ian. I—Mr Donnelly.

IAN: Ian.

BEA: Ian.

IAN: Same name you've used since kindergarten, Bea.

BEA: Just if I get too familiar. Work's not choir, is it?

IAN: Apologies for not turning up on Sunday. Trust you didn't wait too long before you gave up on us.

BEA: Not to worry. Just wanted you movers and shakers to look at something that might make the monument I talked about. An old figurehead we found in storage actually, something my father must have had. Brent took some photos, give people an idea. But that's not what I...

IAN: The door was closed.

BEA: Must have blown open, sorry. Hear that wind. You've got a drop running...

> IAN, *startled, corrects it.*

That's it.

IAN: Er... Our Rotary chapter is undergoing a bit of a change. They're leaning towards a younger, progressive, forward-looking image. I like to think I have a great deal to offer.

BEA: You're certainly into everything. The committee work you do...

IAN: And so I intend to be nominated for President.

BEA: Well, let's hope it doesn't rain, or someone doesn't toss a drink over your head. I'm a bit nervous, truth to tell.

IAN: If this is about Mary's position—

BEA: No.

IAN: As I said, you are being considered—

BEA: It's a bit more serious than that. I've written a letter, you see. Not that I've sent it yet. Because I don't know whether to sign it. It's about Peter Greig. In his capacity as the Dunbar Development Group.

IAN: A letter.

BEA: Everyone knows how much work he does for Dunbar. Building the new Shire nursing home… Trying to attract other business here to replace the oil rigs…

IAN: The new prison if we get it…

BEA: That's what it's about.

    Pause.

IAN: Go on. There's no one around. They've all gone home.

BEA: And then perhaps it isn't all that serious.

    Pause.

IAN: Not everyone in Dunbar thinks Peter Greig dropped out of the sky. A bullying self-promoting little turd is what some people might say. And that the rest of the family's marginally worse.

    Pause.

BEA: I was given some information about him. That he's been receiving money, regularly, and a lot of it, from one of the three companies vying for the prison contract.

    Pause.

IAN: Shit a brick. Really? Peter Greig?

BEA: From the American company. American Detention Industries. In American dollars.

IAN: Why would someone tell this to you, do you think?

BEA: Until last week my friend worked in a bank in… not here, of course. Miles away. Regular deposits. She made copies of the bank statements, which she shouldn't have done, of course…

IAN: Why send them to you?

BEA: Because I'm working here at Council, I suppose. She probably thought I'd know what to do.

IAN: Have you told anyone else about this?

    BEA *hasn't.*

And you've got copies of his bank statements. These transfers in American dollars.

    She nods.

You don't sign it, they'll put it down to someone with a grudge. You sign your letter. The General Manager of this Council is bound to be very interested.

BEA: Now it all makes sense. Those rumours how Peter Greig's promised them the earth if the prison comes here... Over-bidding some people say.

IAN: And all behind closed doors. Free power, roads. A local railway. You wouldn't know. All that and double it if he's on the take.

BEA: He could be in the pockets of the other two contenders, who'd know.

IAN: And what a way to make money, eh? Off the number of prisoners you've got.

BEA: I said to my sister, when I first heard the words 'private' and 'prison' together, I thought it's some sort of joke.

Pause.

IAN: Still. If we don't win this, we'll have nothing.

Pause. BEA *picks up on* IAN*'s tone.*

BEA: True. Very true. That's right.

IAN: But it must be done above board.

BEA: Yes.

IAN: And your friend, your contact, will come forward of course, if needs be.

BEA: No. It's why she passed it onto me. She'd be worried in case of repercussions. Anyway, she's moved up north. Still, the Town Clerk— [*correcting herself*] General Manager, sorry—he'll want to know. Even if there's nothing to it.

IAN: The General Manager'll be at Rotary actually. So I'll have a word on the Q.T. if you like. Tell him to expect your letter.

A siren sounds.

BEA: Someone's escaped.

IAN: No, no. Just a test. First of the month.

BEA: I still get caught out. Silly me.

IAN: Not for much longer.

BEA: No. [*She begins to leave*] Thank you.

IAN: Any time.

BEA: Should I mention our monument idea for the *Harmony*, do you think? Seeing it's Council land. Maybe suggest they hit Peter Greig for a donation.

Pause. IAN *doesn't laugh.*

Or best to keep the two things separate. Best to keep the two things separate.

TRANSITION. Sound of the howling wind.

PAM *and* DICK SHAW *are in their drapery shop.* DICK *is dressing a mannequin in a winter uniform.*

PAM: Back to front, Dick.

DICK: Oh. I was just thinking…

PAM: Then you can price the blazers.

DICK: [*continuing*]… how it doesn't seem any time at all—Andy's first day at school.

PAM: Onwards and upwards, Dick. Let's not dwell.

> *The bell tinkles.* IAN DONNELLY *enters. He is wearing a different jacket—a different day.*

IAN: Hoo. First taste of autumn, eh? Early morning nip around the old ears. Hope I didn't bring it in with me.

PAM: Yes. I was just saying to Dick, wasn't I?

DICK: What's that?

PAM: Fishermen'll be in soon. Wanting their balaclavas. They'd lose their heads if they weren't screwed on with a good wool balaclava or beanie.

IAN: Well. I'm here with my nursing home hat on. The board of the nursing home would like to offer you the contract to supply the uniforms. All the uniforms. For five years. Renewable to ten, I think. All the official hoo-ha'll be in the mail.

PAM: [*pleased*] Well.

> *Pause.*

DICK: Last year wasn't a good year for us.

IAN: No.

DICK: Taken us a while to get back on our feet. You lose your only son, you're never quite the same.

PAM: Still. He didn't leave a wife and kiddies. Something to be grateful for.

IAN: Yes.

DICK: Not so much as an inkling, you know, that there was anything wrong with his heart.

IAN: Thirty-four's too young.

PAM: So this contract really will be a boost.

DICK: He'd had the standard medical only the Christmas before.

PAM: Ian doesn't need to know all this…

DICK: Ian doesn't. No.

IAN: [*to* PAM] Peter Greig and the nursing home board hoped that you'd be pleased.

PAM: We are. And now what with our Kelly coming back to nurse there—

IAN: Won't be long you'll be running the place.

PAM: Won't be long we'll be residents!

IAN: I know what you mean.

PAM: No, Ian, you're looking younger every time I see you. In your face. You do.

IAN: Well. Better get moving and onto my real job. The board hoped you'd be pleased.

PAM: Thank you.

IAN: Don't thank me, I'm just the messenger.

> IAN *extends his hand to* DICK, *who takes a moment to reciprocate.* IAN *leaves. The doorbell tinkles.*

PAM: Good. Very good. This is Peter Greig's way of making amends. He knows now we're not going to be making waves. What's done is done. Everything back to normal.

DICK: For God's sake, Pam.

PAM: Don't for God's sake me.

> DICK *flusters with the mannequin.*

DICK: You wonder what Peter Greig and his brothers said. Toss the Shaws a bone.

PAM: He genuinely thought we'd be pleased.

DICK: Peter Greig and his brothers laughing at us behind their backs.

PAM: We cannot keep living here if you insist on treating that entire family as the enemy! Andrew would not have wanted this! [*Pause*] Life's too short for bitterness. That's what Andrew would have said. Let it go.

DICK: They're the ones have to look into their souls.

PAM: Ours are clean and that's the main thing. Let's get this winter window done.

> *He kneels to do up the shoelaces on the mannequin, or pick up the uniforms.* PAM *reaches out and strokes his hair.*

It's a lovely pattern, Fair Isle. Fair Isle. From the Spanish Armada, shipwrecked themselves on the Shetland Islands. According to the story on the labels. Those were the days, eh…?

DICK: Getting shipwrecked?

PAM: No. Oh, I don't know. When sailors knew how to knit.

> *She gets a smile out of him.*

DICK: He grew into a good man, didn't he? Andy.

PAM: He was. He was ours on loan. A dazzling loan. [*Pause*] God had his reasons for taking him from us. [*Pause*] Oh, here we go. Here comes the rain.

DICK: Batten down the hatches.

PAM: Put it all behind us. Peter Greig's the loser in the long run.

TRANSITION. Lighting change, the sound of the choir.

BEA *plunges into their home, in a whirl.*

BEA: Issie. [*To herself*] Oh, where is she? Issie.

> ISOLA *appears wearing a dressing gown.* BEA *realises that the place is still in a mess.*

ISOLA: What are you doing home?

BEA: I'm only full of news, I'm only swimming with news about what happened to me today. Something I've had my sights set on like a beacon.

ISOLA: You got promoted. Up to Mary's job.

BEA: Isola. Have you only just got up?

ISOLA: Not really.

BEA: I won't waste my breath asking if you've even got so much as one quote from so much as one tradesman…

ISOLA: They gave you Mary's job.

BEA: The bank isn't going to keep that loan opened forever. This town's scrambled with women wanting childcare, grandmothers all with their own lives now. But you need to get in first.

ISOLA: Did you come home to tell me you got promoted to Mary's job?

BEA: Yes. Yes I did. Thanks for asking.

ISOLA: Great. Great news. Really. It's great, Bea. Sorry about the mess. The day just flapped its wings and off it flew. Congratulations. What a surprise.

BEA: Typical Council, no one tells you direct. Ian taps me on the shoulder. Down we walk to Mary's old office, this is his way of telling me, all cleared out now, of course. Barely recognisable. All he says is, 'This'll be yours, starting tomorrow—have the rest of the day off, why not?' All I could think was, my own office. Me. Eight years ago she was fitting bras in David Jones. What have you got on under... ? Show me. What is it?

> ISOLA *takes off her coat to reveal a slinky dress or nightdress, perhaps it's torn in places. It's a piece of clothing that her mother might have worn in the late fifties or early sixties. She pulls a pair of long, slinky gloves out of the pocket of the coat—* 'Da da!'

What on earth are you doing in that? Where's it come from?

ISOLA: It must have been—

BEA: I know whose it must have been, we shouldn't still have any of that.

ISOLA: It's a box full of her things. I found it down at the boatshed.

> ISOLA *moves around the room.*

BEA: St Vincent de Paul took everything—Aunt Sissy arranged it. The blind's wide open, for goodness sake.

ISOLA: [*singing*] Pretty woman, walking down the street...

BEA: What would you want to put these on for?

ISOLA: [*singing*] Petty woman, the kind you like to meet... Growl!

BEA: Isola.

ISOLA: Wasn't she pretty—?

BEA: Issie. You look—unsettled. Your eyes are all...

ISOLA: She was.

BEA: Take-away from Dim's for lunch, special treat.

ISOLA: I'm the exact same size as our mother. In the head, too. There was a hat. The gloves fit like—[*a glove*]. Ba boom. Ba boom.

> *She begins a striptease.*

BEA: Stop that.

> ISOLA *improvises some strip music.*

ISOLA: Just for fun.

BEA: [*grabbing her*] Take it off. Put your own clothes back on—oh bugger St Vincent de Paul, I'll put a rock in it and throw it off the end of the wharf myself.

ISOLA: Am I being disrespectful?

BEA: There wasn't a great deal to respect. I'm going to Dim's, so think about what you'd like please. [*Pause*] For the love of God, will you take those clothes off.

ISOLA: Because I look like her. I do, don't I? Am I like her?

BEA: Only when you're off in dream land.

ISOLA: And you look like our father.

BEA: We are not like either one of them. We are like ourselves. Where's all this coming from, Issie… ?

ISOLA: I can sort of feel how she felt—

BEA: Don't say that—

ISOLA: Feel what she was like.

BEA: Well, how ironic's that, Issie, because as if she ever gave a tinker's cuss what you were like. Anyone who indulges her feelings ahead of an eight-year-old little girl… Think about it.

ISOLA: Exactly my age next month. When she took to her bed and never got up. That's why you worry when I get depressed. Except I'm not. Depressed.

BEA: I don't think that. You're sensitive, that's all. All the more reason to keep yourself strong.

ISOLA: Maybe there's a gene for it. The psyching-yourself-to-die gene.

BEA: I think it's this Ellen you go out with. I don't think she's good for you.

ISOLA: She is.

BEA: How about you help me type another letter, how about that? A stronger letter this time. I've given the Town Clerk—[*correcting herself*] General Manager get it through your head—given him long enough.

ISOLA *doesn't move.*

It's not as if you've got nothing to do. All this is your project [*the house*]. You're in charge of building us a nest. And a place for kiddies for you to mind. Which you can't do when you're off somewhere in another galaxy. Two years. It's why we came back here. And listen carefully. Her mind was as weak as railway tea. She took to her bed, not long after Dad died. And even though she was a mother, she didn't have the will to get up. She allowed herself too many feelings, and proceeded to suck the life out of everyone around her.

ISOLA *looks as if she's plucking up the courage to say something, but stops herself.*

ISOLA: I worry about you too. I do want you to be happy.

BEA: Then please, please get it out of your mind that you're anything like her. Thirty-nine is just a number. One birthday in a long lifetime.

BEA *embraces* ISOLA. *Then, after a moment, she breaks off when she sees* DARCY.

DARCY: I've interrupted. I'm sorry.

BEA: Bathroom's free. Obviously.

DARCY: Actually…

BEA: Yes?

DARCY: In the storage area below the loft down there—where you've put the figurehead back—

BEA: We can't move all that yet I'm afraid, I believe my sister made that clear—

DARCY: There's a little blue rowboat in the corner.

BEA: Yes, it's lovely. If you'll excuse us.

DARCY: Do you think I could use it, if it doesn't leak?

BEA: No, actually. I don't. We're too close to the bar for rowing. The tides and so on. There are currents and eddies out there that experienced fishermen take very seriously indeed.

DARCY: Just to sit in. Just to go out a little bit and drop anchor. Where you can see through to the horizon.

BEA: You must be very used to getting your own way.

DARCY: The opposite.

BEA: Could've fooled me.

DARCY: [*to* ISOLA] You can't quite see past the entrance even if you lean out from the end of the wharf, I need to get a view of the horizon. To practise taking fixes.

BEA: Now I've heard everything.

DARCY: [*explaining, to* BEA] On the stars. Celestial Navigation. [*To* ISOLA] I thought I mentioned it, sorry. You get better practice in a rocking boat.

BEA: That's all done by satellite. Computers.

DARCY: As a fall-back. In a crisis.

> BEA *thinks she's lying.*

ISOLA: What's it they call the stars… ?

DARCY: Heavenly bodies.

ISOLA: I love that. Heavenly bodies.

BEA: Yes. Well. Even I had one of those at one time until gravity got in the way. [*To* DARCY] You use the bathroom. We don't have time at the moment.

DARCY: I'm very grateful.

BEA: Haven't said yes yet.

> DARCY *goes.*

[*Whispering, to* ISOLA] Dear, you're gullible. She'll be out there, surrounded by scuba divers, delivering drugs in plastic bags. I asked her for a lift in her car the other day, pretended she didn't hear.

> *Pause.*

ISOLA: Sometimes when you talk about me, you really mean yourself. Because we didn't come here for me, we came here for your asthma.

BEA: Well at least I was right about that. I'm going to Dim's. Chinese banquet number nine. Then I'll get you to help me word this next letter.

ISOLA: Do you think I have secrets, Bea?

BEA: I just think you need to keep busy.

TRANSITION. Lighting change.

*Roger Oakley as Brent and Janet Andrewartha as Isola in the
1997 Queensland Theatre Company/Melbourne Theatre Company
production. (Photo: Melanie Gray)*

BEA *goes to another part of the space and reads what she's written on the page in a typewriter.*

BEA: [*reading*] 'General Manager… Cullodin Shire Council etcetera… To express… disappointment… Had no response to my letter to you… Possible fraud at the highest level of Dunbar Development Group which purports to represent our town… [*Typing, or writing*] Once again request a meeting…'

> *In another part of the space,* ISOLA *is sitting, still in the nightdress. She wraps her coat more tightly around her as* BRENT *enters in his gun club gear.*

BRENT: What are you up to?

ISOLA: What are you up to?

BRENT: Duck-shooting over at the lakes. Mid-week you don't get the crowds. Make a day of it if you'd like to come.

ISOLA: I've heard you, you know. Crunching around in the leaves outside my window.

BRENT: I've heard you, too. And seen you. Sometimes I can smell you. But I don't mind. I'm prepared to wait.

> *She gets up and leaves.* BRENT *blows her a kiss.*

TRANSITION to BEA's *new office.*

BEA *enters half-running, carrying an assortment of files as if they were stolen. Breathless, she scrambles in her bag for her inhaler. She shakes it, puffs, and inhales. Then she notices* IAN *standing in the doorway.*

BEA: Oh, thank God. Thank God. I couldn't find out if you were away again. Now. There's some sort of a mix-up.

IAN: Is there?

> BEA *has another puff.*

BEA: For three days… I've got nothing to do. I barely slept last night for worrying, truth to tell. I've got nothing to do. I'm waiting to be briefed, you see. To be taken through my job. Look. It's as empty as the day you walked me in here. Except someone put a blind on the window that I can't for the life of me open.

IAN: Let's have a look.

BEA: It doesn't matter. I thought by this morning, well, I'll bring in my old computer and… now that disabled chappie's out there training on it. I can hardly snatch it back.

IAN: [*gesturing towards the files*] I might just take these, if you don't mind.

> BEA, *in a daze, starts to give them to him and stops.*

BEA: You're teasing me, aren't you? You don't even know what's in them.

> *But he takes them all the same.*

IAN: It's okay. Just for the moment.

BEA: You don't. [*Pause*] When I walked past the tea room they seemed to be getting ready for a surprise party. Someone saw me and they all shut up. Perhaps they think I was promoted over their heads. Not realising that I'm qualified. Perhaps I should put my Accounting Diploma on the wall.

IAN: This is only temporary.

BEA: When all's said and done, I'm more of a group person. A group girl. But I can't even go and plonk myself out there, can I? The disabled's got my seat. Well, he's got his own, of course, but…

IAN: I'm not sure I can help.

BEA: You're finance officer, of course you can.

IAN: Sit quietly. Bring in some novels if you like. No one will worry, there won't be any fuss.

BEA: As if I can be paid for reading novels.

IAN: Magazines.

BEA: Will you put that in writing, that I'm to sit in here and form my own private book club?

IAN: Some of us have had to learn to be very cautious about what we put in writing.

BEA: You told me to.

IAN: A Council employee doesn't write a letter like that to the Mayor. Over the head of the General Manager.

BEA: To get a response. What did he say to you, about what's in them?

IAN: Nothing. Only he'd got a letter.

BEA: Three letters I've sent to the Town Clerk—G.M.—you'd almost think he didn't want to know. The Mayor at least will give me a response.

IAN: You know people, Bea. At the first sign of trouble they scuttle back into their holes.

BEA: I'm not trouble.

IAN: I breed canaries as you know, Bea, and often think about how, when miners used to take them underground, and the bird'd start to look a bit green around the gills, how those blokes would've just dropped the cages and ran. No one picking up the little bodies and carrying them up in their pockets. These are delicate times. Thirty-five other shires made submissions to get a prison. Here we are, a breath away.

BEA: So this wasn't a promotion after all.

IAN: Look, I'm all for principles, what you've done is very brave—

BEA: What's brave got to do with it? I'm not brave.

IAN: Well, that's good then. Because you won't do anything foolish.

BEA: So the Greigs and the Town—[*correcting herself*]—G.M. are in some sort of cahoots.

IAN: I didn't hear you say that—

BEA: Those dodgy contracts last year, the nursing home—

IAN: All cleared up now, Bea. I know it is, I'm on the board.

BEA: Who's told you to do this?

IAN: I beg your pardon.

BEA: Someone's told you to do this. Who?

IAN: I just came in here for these files.

BEA: I have in my possession bank statements that look like Peter Greig's been taking regular bribes and the General Manager of Council doesn't even ask to see them. Someone's trying to shut me up.

IAN: I'd say someone just wants you to be quiet for a bit. Tear up the bank statements, forget all about it.

BEA: How can I? How could I do that? The Mayor, surely he'd want to know.

IAN: Twelve months of building work, six hundred prisoners eating eighteen hundred meals a day… A sixty-million-dollar business! The concreting for starters.

BEA: As if I could stop that.

IAN: The surprise in there's for me, actually. I've been elected President of Rotary.

BEA: [*fighting back tears*] You'll need a new repertoire in dirty jokes, then. Ask Babs. She'll tell you a few.

IAN: Which gives me a position on the Development Group. Community representative. I'll be able to keep an eye on things.

    Pause.

BEA: Maybe I rubbed someone's back up with my idea of having a monument. It's not that I want to rake up the past.

IAN: There isn't anything to rake up.

BEA: People might deep down blame our father, but he paid the price… so did we…

IAN: No need to keep on harping about it.

    He starts to go.

BEA: When Issie and I moved back up here after all those years away, the first day we walked up to the shops, and there on the footpath, from the old cash and carry to the hot bread shop, were coins. Covering the footpath in curves and circles and swirling shapes. One dollar coins, two dollar coins. People were pleased to put down their coins. Kiddies. Old people and their pension money. It was to send your wife off for cancer treatment. I thought, that's what people are like in Dunbar. I still think that's what they're like. Not this [*the room*].

IAN: If you don't tear them up, then keep them somewhere safe.

    IAN *leaves.*

TRANSITION to a part of the river bank at night. Water lapping. No wind.

In the half-darkness ISOLA, *laughing, finds* IAN. *A moment of play between them, then they snuggle their way to the ground, and cuddle up looking out at the water.* ISOLA *is dressed in her mother's long satin nightdress, a shawl around her shoulders.*

ISOLA: That's better.

IAN: All we need now is the axe-murderer to come galloping through the trees.

ISOLA: You said my choice.

IAN: Mountain View Motel, Settlers' Motor Inn—that's what that usually means.

ISOLA: We can pretend we're in the scouts together…

She arches up and kisses him.

I bet you were a dear little boy.

IAN: The appendix kid.

ISOLA: What's that mean?

IAN: You know that tired old story…

ISOLA: No. I don't. You must mean someone else.

> *Pause.* IAN *realises that it's his wife who's heard the story ad nauseam. And now* ISOLA *notices—his wedding ring.*

Ian. I shouldn't have to ask.

He takes off the ring and puts it in his wallet.

IAN: Sorry.

> *Pause.*

ISOLA: I want to hear the story.

IAN: You look so pretty. The water's sparkling on your face.

ISOLA: What's the appendix story?

IAN: Okay. It was when my brother, Trevor, was still alive, I didn't want to go somewhere. His football finals or something. So I suddenly had a searing pain in my side.

ISOLA: You were pretending—

IAN: I was indeed.

> ISOLA *laughs.*

So I'm moaning and groaning, and next thing there's a surgeon. And he's saying the situation's very grave, very grave indeed. The appendix could burst at any minute. Next thing I'm whisked away.

ISOLA: So then you said wait, it's an act.

IAN: I didn't have a chance. Plus they'd promised me all this Leggo—

ISOLA: He didn't take out your appendix.

IAN: He certainly did.

ISOLA: [*laughing*] Honestly, Ian, the things that happened to you…

IAN: More than that. More than that. After this emergency operation, the surgeon comes to my bedside. I look at him, he looks at me. Then he tells my parents he caught it in the nick of time. It was just about to burst, he says. Just about to burst. I looked on his face for the flicker of a lie, but there was nothing. Just about to burst.

ISOLA: Did you get your Leggo?

IAN: You bet I did after that. Age of seven, I'd figured out how the world works…

> ISOLA *laughs.*

ISOLA: The things you got up to, Ian… I don't know.

IAN: So pretty when you laugh. I was worried when you phoned. You had that catch in your voice. Upset.

> *Pause.*

ISOLA: I can see Virgo. Look.

IAN: [*the stars*] I can never figure them out—

ISOLA: Darcy, this tenant, showed me. With little Libra chasing behind.

IAN: That's a tampon. Libra. Guess that's where they got the name. The tampon chasing the virgin.

> *He makes a playful galloping gesture down her breasts.* ISOLA *arches up and embraces him. A moment—*

That's what I've been smelling. Mothballs.

ISOLA: This nightdress belonged to my mother. I thought you'd like the feel.

IAN: I do.

ISOLA: It's the sort of thing people leave to their daughters. Then it'll be our luck to have all boys. There was something in the paper about women who have babies at forty. The tests. Which ones. I've kept it.

> IAN *opens a new packet of cigarettes and takes one out with the care of an ex-smoker. Then realises, sighs, and puts it back.* ISOLA *looks at him.*

IAN: Nowhere to brush my teeth.

ISOLA: The river.

IAN: It's like quicksand down there. No big deal. Just that… I've got to be able to clean my teeth.

ISOLA: When we're together you can smoke your head off. I'm working up exactly what to say to Bea. She sort of knows, I think. Still Saturday week, right? Bea'll be home. I checked. [*Pause*] So you need to check. That Carol… And we have to decide exactly where we'll go. I mean in the interim. Before we get a place of our own.

IAN: In terms of the day we talked about.

ISOLA: Yes.

IAN: Carol's big appointment's been put back to next month. With the cancer specialists, the head honchos. So until she's got the all-clear... And frankly, at work, given the muddle we seem to be in with Bea...

ISOLA: No.

IAN: I'm in a fair bit of pressure—

ISOLA: No. This is how people lose each other.

IAN: We all need you to be strong.

ISOLA: We all who?

IAN: She's her own worst enemy. Talk to her.

ISOLA: She won't listen to me. She just sees my mouth moving, that's all.

IAN: She just needs to pull her head in.

ISOLA: I won't have her spoil this.

IAN: Well, she is.

ISOLA: She's all bluff. She comes home from work trembling like a leaf.

IAN: Yeah.

ISOLA: You see that sandy island over there? Bea can't look at it without going white. Some older kids left her there once, years ago—could have been your brother, who knows, this was before the *Harmony* went down—pretended they were all getting off, then snapped the engine in reverse and pulled away. When they brought her back she had to be sedated. Never went on a boat again. Being isolated. Being left alone. She even sleeps with a night light on.

IAN: Really?

ISOLA: Oh yes.

IAN: This information this woman gave her... reckon you can find out where she's got the papers?

TRANSITION. Lights on BEA *staring at her phone, picking at something—a sticker.*

As IAN *crosses the space, she brandishes the receiver.*

BEA: Look at this! Look! 'All outgoing calls from this phone are being monitored.' Someone's put that on there! Tell me, please Ian—what do those women think I've done? Someone's said something to them. You know how in winter you can almost feel the Antarctic? That's what it's like out there.

> IAN *leaves. Sound of the choir singing 'Blow the wind southerly'—a jaunty English folk song.*

TRANSITION. BEA *crosses the space behind* BRENT. *Somewhere there is a pile of copies of the local throw-away newspaper that he runs. He has a fax in his hand that he folds, not wanting her to see.*

BRENT: Bea. I've been meaning to tell you, Bea. The figurehead photos didn't come out, lost the entire roll. Camera might need a service. You look crook, nothing personal. I thought you looked crook at choir.

BEA: I am. Sort of.

BRENT: Something happened to Issie?

BEA: No, Brent. Something's happening to me. I get to sleep these days just in time to wake up again. This is serious. Something for you to publish. That seems to be the best thing to do. Flush it out. It can't get much worse. You wouldn't have to say that I was the source.

BRENT: I'm not with you.

BEA: That envelope I got that other Sunday. It was about a connection between Peter Greig and American Detention. So far I've been pursuing this along all the proper channels, inside Council, but one by one they've all silted up.

> *She hands him a piece of paper.*

Isola helped me word it. So it could sound more natural. As if I was being interviewed.

BRENT: I can't read while you're talking, Bea.

BEA: You'll be able to make it more journalese.

BRENT: [*reading*] Hell. Hell's bells. [*Pause*] Gosh. And that's in American dollars…

BEA: Thousands and thousands. It's a matter of public concern.

BRENT: It is.

BEA: This is news. I don't need to tell you that. And it's your job to print the news.

BRENT: Bea. You know what sort of paper this is. Real estate and yard sales with a good dose of community round-up.

BEA: You said you were changing direction. I've seen your ears burn with anger when they've called you the Council newsletter. [*Pause*] So far I've kept it quiet but... I'm getting further and further out on a very thin limb. It occurs to me now the safest thing is to be noisy. You're the only journalist I know.

BRENT: Who else knows about this?

BEA: Isola. Ian Donnelly. And the General Manager of Council... whoever reads his mail before they hand it on.

BRENT: They're big businesses these prisons. Another ten years they'll be dotted all over the country.

BEA: And the Mayor. It's not in my nature to ask for help, but God help me Brent, I'm stuck in a room with a window that doesn't open, forbidden access to my files, sent to Coventry. They don't like me using the cups. Someone started a rumour I've got Hepatitis C. Isola's upset. Don't think she isn't. She's the one said go to Brent. If Brent knew about this, he'd be shocked. Her words.

Pause. BRENT *sees the opportunity to impress* ISOLA.

BRENT: I am shocked. And if there's something in it, yes...

BEA: Well, doesn't it make you wonder? I'm a middle-aged accounts officer and for some reason they have to send the tanks in.

BRENT: Leave it with me.

BEA: Now we know why the entire Greig family flew off to America for Christmas, eh?

BRENT: I probably wouldn't put that in.

BEA: Making secret deals trying to please the Yanks, using ratepayers' money. If Dunbar wins and they got the contract, who knows what we'll be up for.

BRENT: Yes, well—

BEA: Peter Greig *is* that Development Group. He's got the concrete company, he's got his building outfit... People would really respect you for standing up to them. The city papers might pick this up. You could get a byline or whatever it is.

BRENT: The question I always like to ask myself is whether—

BEA: Whether what? Whether it's time for lunch.

BRENT: Whether it isn't sometimes better to scratch the devil with the fur rather than against it. Just a question. But you leave this with me. Let me run it by our solicitor—

BEA: Stan Whiter? He's in the Development Group!

BRENT: Another one. Tell Isola not to fret, I'll see how much I can publish, what more I can find out.

BEA: Is that your word? [*But* BEA *glances at the window*] Hide that. Quick.

> BRENT *slips the paper under one of the throw-aways.*

So it's quite simple really, Brent. Just take the breath after that and—

> IAN *arrives with some envelopes under his arm, surprised to see* BEA.

Flu or something. Stomach bug. But I think I'll be right by tomorrow.

IAN: I know. Take it easy. [*To* BRENT] This is just Rotary business...

BEA: [*to* BRENT] Well, now you've got a baritone to coach you. [*To* IAN] He's struggling with the middle section. [*To* BRENT] Diaphragm. Palate. See the note as a piece of string.

> BEA *goes. Silence between the two men.* IAN *pulls out some photos.*

IAN: Photographs as requested. The new President of Rotary, my good self. And Pete Greig's got a new mug shot. You might like one for your files. This is just between us, but apparently there's some news coming through.

BRENT: I know.

IAN: You do?

BRENT: I am a newspaper. I am kept informed.

IAN: That the State Government's just awarded the contract to the Yanks, to American Detention Industries.

BRENT: [*the fax in his hands*] And they'll announce which of the shortlisted towns'll get the prison by the end of the month. Embargoed until tomorrow.

IAN: That's right.

> IAN *puts his hand on the first newspaper on the top of the pile.*
> *He looks at* BRENT *carefully, then picks it up. He shakes it, and*
> *out falls the paper from* BEA. *Silence. The piece of paper lies on*

the floor. IAN *picks it up. He waits for* BRENT *to ask for it back, gives him the option. To* BRENT*'s shame, he doesn't. He reads the contents, shaking his head. And puts the paper in his pocket.*

So what do you think public reaction will be?

BRENT: [*struggling to suppress his shame*] The Yanks have got a track record. All those prisons in the South.

IAN: That's right. Still. Embargoed until tomorrow. We don't want to jeopardise anything from here on in. Only one town can win this.

BRENT: That's right.

IAN: Good. [*As if it slipped his mind*] You'll be getting an invitation. For Rotary. I know you tried to join years ago. Some sort of stuff-up, best to forget. It's a very different organisation now. [*Pause*] Stan Whiter proposed you, seconder Ian Donnelly.

BRENT: Thank you.

IAN: You'll enjoy it. We'll enjoy having you. I assume you were intending to tear this [BEA*'s article*] up. [*As he goes*] Less breath on the lower notes. But the next person's always going to tell you something different.

TRANSITION to BEA*'s office.* BEA *with a pile of continuous paper— figures on a print-out. Struggling to make sense of them, she's shaky. Hasn't been sleeping. Determined to perform an impossible task that's been set for her. In her panic, she knocks the pile to the ground. She scrambles to stop it cascading even further.*

DARCY *appears in the doorway.* BEA, *now kneeling, takes a moment to realise who it is.*

BEA: You. Yes. What do you want?

DARCY: Let me give you a—

BEA: Oh my God, something's happened—

DARCY: What… ?

BEA: To Isola. Something's happened, tell me.

DARCY: Hey. Please. Nothing's happened. Everything's all right. She's at home. Nothing's happened.

She reaches in her pocket and pulls out a bottle of pills. She gives them to BEA.

Your blood pressure tablets. Your sister thought you might have been worried.

BEA: Why would she send you?

DARCY: I was dressed, I didn't mind.

BEA: How did you get in here?

DARCY: The girl at the front desk—

BEA: What did you say, she left her medication… is that what you said?

DARCY: Yes.

BEA: Isola wasn't dressed. Is that what you're saying?

DARCY: I'm not sure. Look. She said to remind you to take one at eleven.

BEA *suddenly finds herself with tears in her eyes.*

BEA: Issie said that, did she? Bless her. What I'd do without her, I don't know. Off you go then—ah—!

BEA *has a sharp stabbing pain in the side of her head.*

DARCY: What is it?

BEA: It's a brain tumour. But it's a vast improvement on yesterday's bowel cancer.

DARCY: [*the tablet*] Would you like some water?

BEA: Before you go, just have a look out there for me. See if they're reading the *Chronicle*. It should be out by now.

DARCY: They look like they've been to a meeting.

BEA: No one glancing this way, ashamed?

DARCY: Not really.

BEA: I'm being tested, you see. And I'm not used to failing. I've just found out I'm actually a temporary employee. Something I never realised. Whatever they do I've got no right of appeal.

DARCY: That doesn't sound right—

BEA: It's right! Sorry. I… perhaps I do need to get some water.

DARCY: Sure…

BEA: From the toilets. [*Pause*] Yesterday I nearly wet myself holding on.

DARCY *picks up on this small cry for help.*

DARCY: Well, actually I need to go, too. Maybe you could show me where it is.

BEA: Well. All you needed to do was ask. I can show you. But you can't smoke in there or anything. Just stick close to me. We don't want you bumping into things.

> BEA *steps bravely out into the corridor, followed by* DARCY.

Sound of rain. TRANSITION to DICK *and* PAM SHAW. DICK *shakes water off their umbrella as the rain sound dies.*

PAM: Bea Samson. Don't look. She got caught red-handed stealing money in the Council tea-rooms.

DICK: I don't think that'd be right.

PAM: She's having a nervous breakdown on account of she got caught. They've had to put her in a room by herself. It's why she hasn't been to choir.

DICK: There's always a bit more to it.

PAM: What do you mean by that?

DICK: I just heard she had some information. That no one wants to hear.

PAM: About what?

DICK: I don't know.

PAM: She stole some money. Babs isn't loose with the truth. Why would Babs make up a thing like that? Why would she?

DICK: I'm just saying people say things twice these days and that means they're set in stone… You don't always know what's what.

PAM: You can tell by looking at her there's something very wrong there.

DICK: I wonder people don't say the same about me.

> *Sound of thunder.* PAM *looks up.* DICK *doesn't. They begin to scurry home.*

Sound of thunder and lightning in quick succession. TRANSITION to the house. BEA *takes an uncustomary gulp from a large glass of wine and relishes the storm.* DARCY *looks uncomfortable, out of place.*

BEA: Chain lightning!

DARCY: They were saying that if the wind gets up another few knots it'll stem the tide. So strong the tide won't move.

> *The door slams.* ISOLA *enters. She is surprised to see* DARCY.

Your sister felt like having someone with her.

ISOLA: If you're well enough to entertain, you're well enough to go back to work.

ISOLA *exits immediately.*

BEA: I suppose you probably say to your friends it's odd. Two people living happily together.

DARCY: No.

BEA: What exactly do you do up here? Pop up for a couple of days. Pop back.

DARCY: A retreat. Nourishment.

BEA: Nourishment. Sit outside the boatshed eating seaweed sandwiches or something. Nourishment.

DARCY: In a couple of weeks I... I have to appear before an inquest.

BEA *thinks she's hearing things.*

BEA: Did someone tell you to say that to me?

DARCY: What?

BEA: You repeat what you just said.

ISOLA *re-enters.*

DARCY: Er... that in a couple of weeks I have to appear before an inquest. Um... I should...

BEA: [*to* ISOLA] Can you ask her if that was meant to be some sort of a joke?

ISOLA: Our father shot himself in the mouth the night before an inquest. Oh, hasn't Bea told you that?

DARCY: No...

ISOLA: How striking. Keeping something to herself.

DARCY, *uncomfortable, now waits to find a moment to clarify what she said.*

[*Continuing, to* BEA] Thanks to you, Judith Warren came up to me on the street just now and practically spat in my face.

BEA: She what?

ISOLA: Exactly what I said!

BEA: Tell me what you mean, she spat in your face...

ISOLA: 'Your family's been nothing but trouble in Dunbar. You should never have come back.'

Peter Carroll as Dick Shaw and Judi Farr as Pam Shaw in the 1998 Sydney Theatre Company production. (Photo: Tracey Schramm)

BEA: She said that? How dare she…

ISOLA: A glass of wine, your G.P. said, not the entire crate.

BEA: I won't let anyone harm you.

ISOLA: She meant you, Judith Warren. She meant you're trouble.

BEA: Brent's due here any sec. When tomorrow's *Chronicle* comes out, then the attention won't be on me.

ISOLA: Oh, spare me—

BEA: He's following up all sorts of things—he's been getting somewhere. He has.

ISOLA: I will not be humiliated in the street.

BEA: Once people know the truth—

ISOLA: Who says you know the truth?

BEA: The facts. [*To* DARCY] Make a dash / before it starts to rain.

ISOLA: [*overlapping her*] / Who says you do?

BEA: I do. It's all I have.

ISOLA: She meant right back to the *Harmony* accident.

BEA: I know what she meant.

ISOLA: I told you they still blame us for it. I was a bloody toddler!

BEA: Come and sit down. [*To* DARCY] Third shelf in the bathroom there's a hairbrush. Ta.

> DARCY, *despite herself, goes.*

Issie—and I have had a bit too much—this is just a patch of fog. You were frightened of fog when you were little. The old car'd float above the ground. Through the clouds to the top of the world. Where have we gone, you'd say. Then we'd stick our hands out the windows and show you it was nothing. Just what we were passing through. What you have to know, what you really have to know right to the soles of your feet, is I would do anything, anything to keep you safe. That's what being guardian means.

ISOLA: It does not!

> DARCY *returns with the brush.*

BEA: Thank you.

DARCY: Listen—

ISOLA: [*over her*] For God's sake, Bea. It doesn't mean anything like that—

BEA: All right—

ISOLA: It means look after someone until they've turned eighteen. Help them stand on their own two bloody feet.

A knock at the door.

DARCY: [*to* BEA] I'm sorry about your father, but it wasn't a joke. Okay?

She goes.

BEA: We'll talk about this later.

ISOLA: No we won't.

BRENT *enters.*

BRENT: Greetings. Greetings. Sorry I'm late. Had to go and see my father.

BEA *has to ask...*

BEA: How is he?

BRENT: Recognised me today. Moving into a lucid phase. Can't see the entrance from up here, can you?

ISOLA: No.

BRENT: They say if the wind keeps up it's likely to stem the tide.

BEA: [*distracted*] So Issie said.

ISOLA: I did not. I couldn't care less about the tide.

BRENT: The seas are wearing away at the bar. Someone said they saw the iron ribs of the *Harmony* sticking up out of the sand.

BEA: That's not possible... Someone's been spinning tales.

BRENT: That's what they said.

Pause.

BEA: You better have something to show me, Brent.

BRENT: The bad news is you won't find a story in tomorrow's paper.

BEA: No! Brent! You promised.

BRENT: I'm sorry. But there's a reason for it.

BEA: Here I am been counting the days.

BRENT: Just a bit more investigation to do. And your legal clearance for any accusations...

BEA: If they had the facts... People have abused Issie in the street.

ISOLA: I don't care.

BEA: Tell him what that Judith Warren said.

ISOLA: Just drop it.

BEA: How much of the boat can you see?

BRENT: Hard to say. Visibility's low.

Pause.

BEA: If you can't help me, Brent, you say now.

ISOLA: That's right, Brent. Just say.

BRENT: Look, there's a long trail of petrol leading very close to Peter Greig.

BEA: Until it all goes public…

BRENT: Just at the moment the wick's all in little pieces—

BEA: My head…

BRENT: Well perhaps this is giving you time to reconsider. If you want to pursue this.

BEA: What's the alternative… ?

BRENT: To let it drop.

Pause.

BEA: I'm wedged between the rocks.

BRENT: Once I assemble the facts about Peter Greig, enough facts to avoid a defamation suit…

BEA: Yes.

BRENT: Otherwise you go in half-cocked, excuse the language, and they dig up all sorts of dirt against you.

ISOLA: Why did you look at me when you said that?

BRENT: I didn't.

BEA: Hello, lover's quarrel.

ISOLA: Shut up—

BEA: Just joking, Miss Snappy.

BRENT: Lightning again.

ISOLA: Give me an umbrella with a metal tip. I'll go and stand outside.

ISOLA begins to leave.

BEA: I can't just keep taking time off…

BRENT blocks ISOLA's way.

BRENT: [*to* ISOLA] You ignore that Judith Warren.

Pause. Then ISOLA *leaves the room.*

BEA: You're still doing it, Brent. The way you looked at Issie just now. Don't look at her like that.

> *Pause.*

BRENT: Well. Even if you drop all this right now, you can't say you haven't given the powers-that-be a shake-up.

BEA: A shake-up. What use is that… ?

BRENT: Sometimes, I think that the other kids who got on the boat that day and drowned were the angels among us. And somehow, when they went, the parents, the survivors, everyone in Dunbar all toughened up. All grew plates of skin. What was good sort of slipped out into the currents and something hidden came in from the sides in its place. [*Pause*] What you've done is broken their seal.

> *Pause.*

BEA: Just because this is slippery and subtle, mustn't mean it can't be dealt with. But if you don't want to, tell me. You really are working on this story.

BRENT: Wasted hours if I pulled up now…

BEA: You're not just trying to get in with the big boys.

BRENT: Ah well, Bea, if this is how you treat your friends.

BEA: You talk about being a kid. When you were a kid I could never get you. You hated the big boys for every meanness and hurt, but you busted yourself desperate to play with them. Maybe you're still like that.

BRENT: You're the one asked me for help. I'll forget you've said all this.

BEA: I don't know who to trust. People's eyes aren't leading to their hearts.

BRENT: They do say you know when you're being effective by the strength of your enemy's dirty tricks.

TRANSITION to the choir. Assembled as it was before, they begin in the middle of 'O Waly Waly'. They sing two or three bars, stop and repeat. This happens a number of times until BRENT *catches on and sings the correct notes.*

BEA's voice is choking her. She is, unseen by anyone else, becoming more and more upset. She takes a puff from her inhaler and as the rest of the choir sings through, she's consumed by wheezing. She gestures to ISOLA *that she's fine, not to follow her and starts to leave.*

Suddenly, a wheely-bin lurches onto the space and crashes, spilling garbage. The choir stops. BEA *steps forward.*

TRANSITION. Night, outside BEA *and* ISOLA*'s house. As* BEA *picks up the garbage, she fights back tears.* ISOLA *enters.* BEA *sees her but gets that sort of fright where the scream is already in her throat. She screams.*

BEA: Ah! Oh God, sorry. I didn't mean to frighten you. How did you get home?

> ISOLA *doesn't answer. She just looks at the garbage.*

I didn't hear a car, that's all.

ISOLA: I got dropped off on the corner. Ian Donnelly gave me a lift. As a matter of fact.

BEA: Didn't dare look my way once, all choir. He didn't say anything to you, I hope.

ISOLA: Carol is refusing to have her final tests, to give her the all-clear from the cancer.

BEA: You know what I mean.

ISOLA: What are you doing?

BEA: Someone has strewn our garbage all over our front lawn. [*Picking it up and holding out an eggplant*] We really should stop buying eggplant. Or figure out how to cook it… I'm not sure what to do, Issie.

ISOLA: Leave it 'til morning. Bea…

BEA: Wait. I'm going to have to tell you something. Sergeant stroke Councillor Kevin Simons pulled me over, coming home. And after he'd stuck his leathery old face in the window, though why he wanted to see my licence who would know—

ISOLA: Because you did something, obviously. You can freeze to death, I'm not.

BEA: And when I looked up he'd pulled out his gun. Now. Just on the way home. He held his revolver this far from my head. Leaning it on the door. A gun. Once you've seen what a firearm can do… it's the mess on a wall, it's the bits and pieces. No one ever talks about that…

ISOLA: Are you sure you—?

BEA: It was this far from my head. All I could see was this black metal. Filling the window. He says, 'I heard something. Ssssh. What was that?' Asked me if I heard something. Then he said, 'Oh well. Must have made a mistake.' But he takes such a long while before he put away that gun. And said something very pointed about looking a gift horse in the mouth. [*Pause*] He put the Stretka boy in hospital.

ISOLA: The Stretka's boy was a drug addict.

BEA: Who would I report it to?

ISOLA: No one.

> *Pause.*

BEA: But you believe me.

ISOLA: I can see that you're very shaken.

BEA: Anyway. I see a specialist tomorrow in Alderton. Get the all clear to go back to work.

ISOLA: That's good.

BEA: Go inside, I'm sorry to worry you.

> ISOLA *starts to go in, then turns.*

ISOLA: Have you got those papers somewhere safe? You should.

BEA: Underwear drawer. A pantyhose packet.

ISOLA: You haven't made any copies?

BEA: You know that board that's so loose you can get your hand behind it? Lower down the wall, there's a ridge, a sort of a shelf.

> *Depending on the set,* BEA *can alternatively say: 'You know that board that's so loose you can get your hand beneath it? The joist's a sort of a shelf.'*

This'll all sort itself out.

> ISOLA *starts to go.* BEA *blows kisses—their nightly ritual.*

Sweet dreams.

> *But* ISOLA *doesn't respond.*

TRANSITION. Lighting change. The office corridor.

IAN *enters, followed by* BEA *who is washed out, weary, almost in shock.*

BEA: Stop please, Ian. Stop. I have to know who pinned that up on the noticeboard.

IAN: What does it matter?

BEA: It's a psychiatric report!

IAN: Keep your voice down.

BEA: The whole world read it. This is trying to erode me, wear me into the ground…

IAN: You might be best to go home.

> BEA *has a piercing pain in her stomach.*

BEA: Take no notice. Just giving birth. Oh boy…

IAN: I'll have a word with them—

BEA: I demand you find out who pinned that up.

IAN: It was a practical joke—God knows you've pulled a few—

BEA: No one said he was a psychiatrist. They said go to Alderton and see this other doctor before you come back to work…

IAN: Well, clearly you need some help. You're certainly not fit to be at work. Hurry up and get your bag, and I'll slip you out.

BEA: It's confidential information!

IAN: Look, you've done enough damage—upsetting staff—get yourself home.

BEA: Sniggering. Babs was sniggering. Tell me, Ian—what do those women think that I've done?

IAN: The average person likes things to run on an even keel.

BEA: They're not—

IAN: Well, they might if people just focussed on their own lives.

BEA: I don't like being lied to.

IAN: Heck, Bea. Who does?

BEA: Even before I walked into that man's office, someone had told him that I was either mad or dangerous. He seemed quite disappointed I didn't rip my clothes and kneel in my undies with a bobby pin stuck in a power point. It wasn't until I checked his certificate—He saw me doing it. I suppose that's in there. Paranoid.

> *She reaches for the report, but* IAN *doesn't let her have it.*

IAN: You're going home, you're writing a letter to the Mayor. CC it to the General Manager, assuring them you made a mistake. Suspicion unfounded and so on.

BEA: Something here… there's something here… something here not right with people…

IAN: I'm trying to help you, Bea.

BEA: I'm not the one with a disease!

IAN: Did you hear what you said?

BEA: Someone says I'm poison and it's no questions asked. What is wrong with these people! I walk up the street, I've seen eyes glaze over!

IAN: Drive. Take the taxi.

BEA: Sweeping dirt under the carpet doesn't disappear the dirt. And I'll tell you something—I reckon that if American Detention said they were looking for a town to send prisoners to the moon, Peter Greig'd be falling over himself to set up a space program using ratepayers' money.

IAN: The truth is, Bea… no one's going to die from it.

BEA: Read it out.

IAN: You're not meant to see this—

BEA: Everyone else has. I have a right to know!

IAN: Okay, okay, you want to know? [*He reads the report*] 'Fixated by an imagined injustice… Neurotic reaction unless things go her way. Suspect personality disorder… Requires further testing. Presents as fearful she will take her own life in the manner of her father. That her sister will succumb to depression in the manner of—'

BEA: That isn't what he asked me!

IAN: [*poised to continue*] It goes on.

BEA: I have such pain in my stomach I'm surprised you can't feel it.

IAN: Call your doctor when you get home.

BEA: No, he's likely to give me arsenic. Or worse. Or maybe it's sprinkled on there.

She tries to take the report before he folds it up.

IAN: You're becoming your own worst enemy.

BEA: Well, you lick it then. I dare you. Taste it! Ha! I will not go home. I'm going to sit outside the General Manager's office until he agrees to see me. I don't care if I sit there all night.

IAN: The most intelligent thing for you to do is sign something to say you've just found out that your source of information, that this person you know, was deliberately making mischief. You got caught in the middle.

BEA: You said that, Ian! But it isn't the truth!

IAN: All right, not mischief then. Not mischief. Full-scale chaos! How's that sound? Look at yourself, your health's in a mess, I don't even know what you're doing in here—

BEA: I can't just pretend, how can I just pretend—?

IAN: Just write a letter saying the documents you were given were fraudulent.

BEA: They're not—

IAN: They might be—

BEA: There must be more going on and they assume I know—

IAN: All in your mind, all in your mind—

BEA: So why the scud missiles trained on my head!?

IAN: Co-incidence!

BEA: And what do you think it would make me, if I wrote such a letter?

IAN: I don't know—

BEA: I'm trying to see who you are.

IAN: Busy, busy's who I am…

BEA: Tell me—what does it make me, if I did that? If I wrote such a letter.

IAN: What sort of inconsiderate, single-minded idiot does it make you if you don't?

IAN leaves her.

TRANSITION. Another part of the offices. ISOLA *is waiting.*

IAN: [*to* ISOLA] She's locked herself in the toilets. My guess is she's going mad. Refuses to talk to a doctor.

ISOLA tries to sneak a kiss but IAN *moves away.*

The female population of the finance section is having to walk two floors up for a wee. Do me a favour and get her out.

Lighting change. ISOLA *steps over to where* BEA *is crouched.*

ISOLA: Ian said, Ian Donnelly said come and get her, she's been in the toilet all afternoon, and her puffer's run out. He thinks you're going mad.

BEA: Maybe I am... [BEA *pulls at her hair—it's falling out. She runs it through her fingers and lets it fall*] I should have saved it. I'll be able to stuff a mattress. Hair won't grow on busy thoroughfares... one of our relatives used to say that...

ISOLA: I do not know, I don't remember. You're causing me a lot of trouble, Bea.

BEA: We don't want that.

ISOLA: We don't. You're casting broken glass around you and then you wonder why I've got bleeding feet.

BEA: I can't have that.

ISOLA: You can't. [*Pause*] What the hell does it matter to you what Peter Greig does?

BEA: It's everyone else I'm wondering about.

ISOLA *is distracted by a letter on the floor.* ISOLA *picks it up.*

No, no. Put it back there. Someone slipped it under the door before.

ISOLA: I want to see.

BEA: [*taking it*] No. You don't know who it's come from.

ISOLA: If you hadn't blabbed your life to the psychiatrist—

BEA: He asked me. How did your parents die? I told him. [*Reading*] Oh my... oh my...

ISOLA: Who's it from?

BEA: It doesn't say. A sort of angel. Peter Greig's done something else. This is it. This is all I need. He's stolen money from the Shaws from choir. Stolen from Andrew, their son, who died last year. Someone else. It's all I need. Someone else.

She passes the accompanying letter to ISOLA.

Out of the valley of the shadow... You must bring me luck, Issie. Lifting me out of the fog. This will all turn out for the best, it will. All it takes is a little spark.

ISOLA *continues to read.*

END OF ACT ONE

ACT TWO

Sound of rain. DICK *is tying neck ties around his neck, and placing them around the collars of a couple of mannequins in uniform. He also has a measuring tape around his arm.* PAM *enters carrying an armload of balaclavas, she holds one up.*

PAM: What do you think? Eh? Bring on the tuna! [*Taking it off*] She's done a nice job, as usual.

> *Knocking, perhaps distorted, on a glass door.*

DICK: Oh. It's Beatrice. Bea Samson.

PAM: She has definitely had a nervous breakdown. Mind you, that family, who'd be surprised?

DICK: [*focussed on the door*] I wouldn't have thought she'd—

> *He breaks off, then gestures towards the door.*

We can't…

PAM: She's having psychiatric treatment.

> *Another knock.* DICK *gives a wave ('Hold on') and continues to the door.*

Tell her we've closed the till. And that the family silver's all hidden under the house. Don't let her—

> *But there is the sound of the door's tinkling bell as* BEA *enters, followed by* DICK.

Oh, it's Beatrice. Sorry, Beatrice. We thought, it's one of the old prison visitors, no idea of time half of them.

BEA: Don't worry, no one saw me walk in. Apparently there's a particularly lethal smell about me at the moment. Put away any young kittens. Lock up your bonsai.

PAM: Well. That's no good.

BEA: No. [*Pause*] I didn't know your son really. Andrew.

PAM: He would have been a toddler when you all moved away.

BEA: I saw him to nod to, of course. Since we came back.

PAM: Yes. Well, we're expecting our daughter home for a visit shortly.

She's working back here. The nursing home.

DICK: Not tonight, Pam.

PAM: What?

DICK: Tomorrow.

BEA: Lately I've been thinking about the moment before a person's stoned to death. They look around. They must think somewhere in this crowd, one of these faces—someone will run forward and get in the way and all the arms will lower and all you'll hear is little thuds as everyone opens their fingers and drops their stones. At work, someone got an envelope to me. About what they've done to you. About your son.

PAM: You don't look at all well.

BEA: The whole story was written out, point by point. How until he passed away he was working for Enderby Holdings. One of the Greig's brother's companies. The one that went into receivership when the offshore rigs dried up. They thought very highly of your son—

DICK: They thought so highly they gave him a bonus.

PAM: Dick…

BEA: A life insurance policy was the bonus. Andrew's life was insured for one hundred thousand dollars—

PAM: We wouldn't know what you're talking about—

BEA: And even though it was his insurance, all that's ever been passed onto you was ten thousand dollars. I think you know about this.

PAM: Call her sister. She'll be wondering where you are.

BEA: The insurance company paid the Greigs and, quite simply, they didn't pass it on. And by the time you realised, and asked about the policy—

DICK: I did that—

PAM: [to DICK] Shut up. [To BEA] We're closed.

BEA: [continuing]—the company had folded—

DICK: That had nothing to do with him.

BEA: —the company had folded and the money was gone. To pay off creditors. I've got copies of the insurance company's correspondence to you, someone got them to me anonymously which was pretty fucking courageous—

PAM: Get out.

Judi Farr (background) as Pam Shaw and Noni Hazlehurst as Bea in the 1998 Sydney Theatre Company production. (Photo: Tracey Schramm)

BEA: The form he signed. Your son. What's it called?

DICK: Nomination of Benefactors.

PAM: We don't know anything about this!

BEA: Counter-signed by Peter Greig. It says, mother—Pam Shaw; Richard Shaw, father—proportion of benefits one hundred per cent. You were grieving and the Greigs—

PAM: We still are, we'll never stop—get out! You're mad.

DICK: [*to* PAM] All right, don't upset yourself.

BEA: They stole from you, and they stole from your son. God knows what else he's done. Peter Greig. I think he's been taking bribes for years. And the Council turns a blind eye.

DICK: That's the way I'm starting to think…

PAM: No you're not. Be quiet.

BEA: A proper enquiry and he'd probably go to gaol. If the three of us got advice, went public. You could get a lawyer to speak on your behalf…

PAM: This is what you need to know. Our only son sat down on the beach last year at the age of thirty-four and his heart stopped.

DICK: He was born a blue-baby, but at three months old he had a clean bill of health.

PAM: He said, 'I'm off for a walk, Mum.' The door slammed with the wind. He walked. He sat down on a rock. His heart stopped and we lost him.

BEA: They're trying to make out I'm mad.

PAM: You are.

BEA: One of you must have sent these to me. Thinking, oh well, she's got her head stuck up so another quoit round her neck won't hurt.

PAM: Have you got these papers, this envelope with you?

BEA: No.

PAM: Then go and tear them up, if you've got any decency you'll tear them up, burn them.

BEA: It's my sister I'm worried about. She's getting more and more depressed at all that's happening to me.

PAM: We've just got to the stage where we can pretend that our son's on a trip somewhere. Where there aren't any stamps.

Pause.

DICK: You might have guessed we're not the sort of people to go jumping around on roof-tops.

BEA: But you want me to jump on your behalf.

PAM: We want nothing of the sort. There are no rooftops. You forget you spoke to us. All we want is to live in peace.

BEA: So I've made another mistake.

PAM: A doozy. [*As she leaves, to* DICK] Dick, show her out.

> DICK *shows* BEA *to the door. She steels herself to go out into the street.* PAM *has gone.*

BEA: [*to* DICK] The word 'anonymous' is a very poor mask.

DICK: The thing is, you're doing what other people can't. It shows them up. People feel a sense of shame, you see. Hostility. All that. Just remember that they're afraid of you. You have more power than you think.

BEA: [*laughing*] No, no. No one's afraid. It's pretty much open season.

DICK: Of how much you know.

BEA: Well I don't. That's why— [*one last try*] even if you just spoke to Brent Bailey at the *Chronicle*—the city papers pick these things up.

DICK: You're a fool if you trust Brent Bailey. Let me just say that much.

BEA: What… ?

DICK: Look, from the minute you moved back here, there've been some people who've been anxious. Of what you might say about the *Harmony*. What's she going to come out with? That's all I'm saying.

BEA: What would I come out with?

PAM: [*offstage, calling*] Dick.

BEA: What?

DICK: You must know all this…

BEA: I don't.

DICK: The whole sorry business after.

BEA: What?

DICK: A proper inquest would have torn this place asunder. And Mr Bailey Senior, if he hadn't lost his nerve.

BEA: Mr Bailey was kind to Dad. He came to our house morning and night.

DICK: I'm just saying it's all entwined. The mess you're in. That wretched boat. What you've found out about our son.

PAM: [*offstage, calling*] Dick.

DICK: It's written in everyone's shadows. But you only see it if you turn around.

> PAM *returns. Conscious of her,* DICK *shows* BEA *out. The sound of the tinkle of the bell.*

PAM: She's just as likely to throw a rock through the plate glass. We're getting blinds. Then once we're shut, we're shut.

> *Silence.*

What were you saying to her?

DICK: That a mistake's been made. Wires have been crossed.

PAM: Someone obviously thinks we're made of steel. That they've got a right to drag back all our pain. [*Pause.* PAM *is certain that it was* DICK *who contacted* BEA.] Perhaps some busy-body from the insurance company contacted her. From when we first made enquiries. [*Pause*] Well, what a hurtful thing is all I've got to say. How very, very hurtful. I won't say what I'm thinking. The words would stick to these walls.

DICK: It's clearing up. I might go for a wander.

PAM: [*taking off her apron*] Oh, all right…

DICK: On my Pat Malone.

> PAM *is taken aback.* DICK *doesn't go for walks on his own. And he does just that, and goes.*

TRANSITION. A blast of car horns and sirens from the bush fire brigade etc. fill the air. This is the beginning of a spontaneous celebration that continues through this scene.

BEA *is writing savagely with a felt-tipped pen. The writing is large, quickly filling pages of her foolscap-size diary.* ISOLA *enters during this.*

BEA: Tuesday. Nearly weep for joy because a new pleasant young man talked to me in the corridor. Turned out he was just delivering the water bottles. Left work Wednesday, two p.m., after only one day there, with more mysterious pains shooting up into my head. On the way out make big mistake. Tell Ian Donnelly that if they dismiss me for having time off... I'd never have the strength to fight it. [*To* ISOLA] Don't use the phone, ABC Radio might be calling me back.

She watches more of her hair fall through her fingers to the floor.

ISOLA: They've been going to call back all week. And you've been holding up the phone all morning so never mind telling me not to—

BEA: Because we had a letter from the bank manager foreclosing on our loan. A hundred calls it took to find out it was a 'mistake'.

A siren whoops. The noise builds. ISOLA *looks out.*

Oh good. I thought for a moment that that [*the noise*] was all in my head.

ISOLA: It's the beginning of a celebration. We got the private prison. Dunbar is the chosen site. It just came on the news. And do you think there's a soul here who could care less what's been promised, as long as Dunbar's won?

In another part of the space, BRENT *picks up a golf club.*

BEA: [*to* BRENT] Local paper arrived this week as usual. With an editorial that read like a Southern Baptist sermon. Warning off trouble-makers trying to stop progress. You meant me.

BRENT: If you want to read it like that.

BEA: 'These are make or break times after all.' But not the way you mean. No. We've broken like a bone china cup with hairline fractures. All perfectly intact, until you pick it up.

TRANSITION. Early morning light, sound of birds. And the sound of the thwack of golf balls. IAN *joins* BRENT *on a driving range.* IAN *surveys the morning.*

IAN: Won't the local tradesmen be falling over themselves today? Let the tendering begin, eh? Makes a man wish he'd gone into the fencing game. Greigy's got the concreting sewn up, but that peripheral fence runs a good few kilometres. Then you've got all the internal fences. And when it's up and running... well. A man could do a lot worse than work for the Yanks.

BRENT: Yep. It's a big day all right. About time Dunbar got on the map.

IAN: A big day. Hear that?

BRENT: What?

IAN: The sound of mobile phones connecting right across the country. Local business'll want to get in quick to collar the work. Firms locking horns. American Detention sitting up waiting for them to wear each other lower and lower down into the pit.

>*Pause.* BRENT *doesn't look at* IAN.

BRENT: It was never in doubt, was it?

IAN: What?

BRENT: That we'd get it? Once American Detention was appointed?

IAN: Why would you say that?

BRENT: The word is they've been promised the earth to come here. Literally the earth. The whisper is we've given them the land.

>*Pause.*

IAN: Now, who'd say that, I wonder?

BRENT: After the Rotary meeting… you know. You hear things said.

IAN: Brent, if I owned a shitty little throw-away country newspaper full of ads for ten cents off a packet of Surf and frozen chickens as illustrated or weekly round-up what's on at the C.W.A. or crap prose from the mouth-frothing fringe of the gun lobby, I'd be starting to think, gee I'd fancy going into colour. Gee, I'd like to see every colour edition hermetically sealed in a plastic bag. As opposed to some competitor opening up to take advantage of the Shire's sudden spring into the twenty-first century. I'd be thinking of being diplomatic, circumspect, and looking at the first edition of real estate in colour. Bigger shitty throw-away papers. Colour. Plastic bags. If you don't know what I mean, have another gander at your excellent editorial. These are make or break times.

BRENT: I think you misunderstood me.

IAN: Did I? That'd be right. What a bloody dill.

>*They go. Cockatoos squawk overhead.*

>BEA *runs on in a panic. She has her underwear drawer dangling from her hands, some items of clothing spilling onto the floor. She lets it fall to the ground and begins to feel beneath a floorboard (or a weatherboard on the wall) for some papers she has hidden. She's in this awkward position when she notices that* DARCY *is watching.*

BEA: You're here.

DARCY: Yes.

> *Pause.*

BEA: Have you been snooping around in here?

DARCY: God no. Of course not.

BEA: Did you go out and leave the back door unlocked? Someone might have asked you to—will you look at me please while I'm speaking to you.

DARCY: No. I just drove up. I just arrived—

BEA: If we're not here and you come in to use the bathroom, you lock the door when you leave.

DARCY: I know…

BEA: Someone has been in here fossicking through my underwear drawer. Did someone ask you to do that for them?

> *Both are distracted by a whoop of the old prison siren we heard earlier.*

Testing the siren at the old gaol. First of the month. Unless it's going up in flames. Water pressure's something shocking up there on the hill.

DARCY: I know what you think.

BEA: You don't look people in the eye.

DARCY: You think I have a boyfriend in the gaol. That that's why I come up to Dunbar. It's not. [*Pause*] You remind me of someone, that's all. It's not my intention to be rude.

BEA: Your arms are longer than mine. It's an envelope.

> DARCY, *puzzled, follows* BEA *to the weatherboard.* DARCY *tries to feel around for the papers.*

Can you find it?

DARCY: No.

BEA: I'll get the kitchen tongs.

DARCY: Yes, yes, I've got it. Yes.

> DARCY *drags a dusty, large envelope up to the surface.*

BEA: Oh, thank God. Thank God. Always keep copies. At least I'm doing something right.

DARCY *starts to go.*

So you're saying you don't have a boyfriend in the clink.

DARCY: No.

BEA: But there's something going on. This… this inquest matter.

DARCY: It's in three days time. In the city.

BEA: Which means someone died. In unusual circumstances. [*Pause*] Who do I remind you of?

DARCY: Someone died. Yes. It's very strange… I… You have to say, I killed a woman.

BEA: It's strange, is it? Well, isn't that a relief. At least it's not every day. Get the milk, buy the bread, kill someone. You unnerve me.

DARCY: It was in a car. An accident, I hope. I've had to get away from things, steel myself for this inquest. The outcome. There'll be witnesses I don't know about. And so on. And if you really want to know…

BEA: Was it your fault?

DARCY: I don't think it was. But if it's… if I get charged with manslaughter, well… then that must be what happened. At first all I wanted was just to get off, start again, but you're not entitled to wish for that really. Even if it goes against me, you can only really hope for the truth. Can't you?

Pause.

BEA: Why did you choose this house?

DARCY: For the boatshed, like I said. I realise I've been in the way— I've heard some of what's been going on—

BEA: You didn't know anybody at all in Dunbar.

DARCY: No.

BEA: Who do I remind you of?

DARCY: You look like her. A lot. This woman. She looked a lot like you. The first time I saw you I… Julia Pender was her name. I've asked your sister. No relation. And so when I was here, answering your sister's ad, you walked in the door.

BEA: Do you have witnesses?

DARCY: It was Saturday afternoon outside the markets. My memory is that she ran straight at the car, I think there was nothing I could do but pull up. Some people stepped forward and told the police exactly that. But there might be others you see, others I don't know about. She flew through the air, over the bonnet… and in that moment… it's strange. I cared for her in that moment more than I've cared for anyone in my life. Also fascination as she soared past. Then she was dead. Ever since I learnt to drive, that's the thing I've been most afraid of. And it's happened. So that's why I didn't give you a lift that day, pretended I didn't hear you. At the moment I'm still scared of myself. [*She pulls a ring out of her pocket*] I found this on the track down near the boatshed. Maybe someone has been snooping around. But it wasn't me. Okay? [*The ring*] 'To Ian, love from Carol.' Unless it fell out of one of the boxes.

> BEA *sits down, in shock. Then suddenly she opens the envelope to look at the papers. She riffles through them, puzzled. Then gasps as she tips them onto the floor.*

They're all blank.

BEA: Taken my originals. Taken my copies. And left me these.

DARCY: I swear to you I didn't leave that door unlocked.

> ISOLA *enters.*

[*To* ISOLA] Something's happened.

BEA: Must be nerve-racking being Peter Greig's lackey. That's all I can say. [*To* DARCY] Don't you worry, this is not your fault—

ISOLA: Who?

BEA: He left his ring behind. Ian Donnelly. Here. Rifling through our things. He took these. I'll… I'll tell them they've beaten me. And could I go back to work as if… as if nothing ever happened.

ISOLA: Good idea.

BEA: Because really, so what if they did get Peter Greig? Someone else would step into his shoes like that.

ISOLA: That's right.

BEA: But then I think, well what does it make my life if I lie too? A joke really. Doesn't it? Signifying nothing.

> ISOLA *picks up the ring.*

And you can't clear your name just by bleating it into the wind. You think you've worked out how the world works, then you haven't got a clue. Issie.

ISOLA: What?

BEA: That time Judith Warren practically spat in your face. Was there anything she said? About our father?

ISOLA: Only mad people knit through their past like this—

BEA: I think it's why they thought they could come down on me like a ton of bricks.

> ISOLA *has slipped the ring on her finger.*

ISOLA: [*to* DARCY] What were you doing giving this to her?

DARCY: I found it.

BEA: Her? Who's her?

ISOLA: You forget about this, Bea.

BEA: It's a criminal offence. I'll take it back to him, dangle it in front of his nose. Tell him he's lucky I don't have him charged.

ISOLA: You're not going to the police, you're not going up to his house—

> DARCY *tries to slip away, but* ISOLA *grabs her.*

[*To* DARCY] Tell her you're making it up, tell her you didn't find it.

BEA: Enough, Issie.

> BEA *grabs* ISOLA. *They struggle.*

ISOLA: Ow.

BEA: Take it off. It's evidence.

ISOLA: Evidence.

BEA: He's stolen all my papers!

ISOLA: You're driving me mad, you're ruining my life!

BEA: I have been subjected to a great injustice and—

ISOLA: You! You! Oh you have, have you—you have—

BEA: Calm down—

ISOLA: Go stuff yourself, you ugly old cow.

> BEA *releases* ISOLA, *shocked.*

I'm stopping you from making a fool of yourself. There'll be another one soon. He's wearing a three-dollar substitute from Woolies, shows how much notice she pays.

DARCY: Oh God.

BEA: What?

ISOLA: You heard.

*Celia Ireland (left) as Darcy and Noni Hazlehurst as Bea in the 1998
Sydney Theatre Company production. (Photo: Tracey Schramm)*

DARCY: I should have just kept it, shouldn't I?

BEA: You mumbled, missy. Tell me what you said.

> ISOLA *is on her feet, the ring in one hand, the other hand on the hem of her skirt.*

ISOLA: I said I'll put it somewhere where he'll be sure to find it later.

DARCY: God.

> *She crouches, begins to put her hand up her skirt, intending to slip the ring inside herself.* BEA *dashes to her to stop her, they struggle again.* BEA *manages to get the ring from her.*

BEA: There is an infection come into this house. My sister isn't well. What a filthy thing to do.

DARCY: Perhaps it's me—

ISOLA: [*to* DARCY, *laughing*] Such crap. She knew all along. [*To* BEA] You knew.

BEA: All along what.

ISOLA: Who's this girlfriend I have dinner with?

BEA: Ellen. She's a teacher. She's—

DARCY: Stop.

ISOLA: Funny she's never phoned, never popped by. Never come here instead of me going all the way to her place twice a week.

BEA: Because we're not set up for visitors…

> DARCY *catches* BEA's *eye and slips away.*

DARCY: I'm sorry.

BEA: [*to* DARCY] Wait. Do you know what she means?

> DARCY's *gone.* BEA *thrusts the ring into her bra.*

I don't understand.

ISOLA: Yes you do.

BEA: This is a dream. My head's floating off…

ISOLA: I wasn't going to tell you like this.

BEA: My God, Isola. How long has this been going on?

ISOLA: I was going to sit you down and—

BEA: So that's why nothing gets done, is it? That's why we live in the shadows of all these promises we made. Because you've been so busy. One foot at the front door, and your fanny pointing up the hill to his place. We don't have secrets, Issie. You can tell me anything!

ISOLA: Except what's important! Except this! You want me in a shoe-box that's got holes punched into the top for air. I can't get enough to breathe.

Sound of a firework in the distance. Just one.

This is very hard for me.

BEA: For you? Oh, spare my days. Use your noggin, Issie. He's not going to leave her.

Another firework.

ISOLA: They're having fireworks tonight to celebrate getting the prison. They're expecting a very big turnout.

BEA: You see, now there'll be no stopping them.

ISOLA: Well. Now will you finally shut up?

BEA: Yes. Yes I will, Issie. If that's what you want, yes. If you stop seeing him, I will do that.

ISOLA: I can't.

BEA: You make me sick to look at you. He's married, Issie, for heaven's sake.

ISOLA: And you think I am. To you.

BEA: Where are your morals?

ISOLA: Same place as everybody else's, I don't know. You hold me down, you don't think you do—

BEA: Obviously you needed to be—

ISOLA: You can't see me. Who I am.

BEA: I will. Tell me. I will. If I've been too interfering, I take that on the chin. That can change. [*Pause*] Who did take all the papers?

ISOLA *groans.*

For God's sake, Isola. You've been here watching me day by day dragging myself out of a rabbit trap, wiping the blood out of my eyes—

ISOLA: I'm sorry.

BEA: When we were apart, when we were doing our own thing—I'd be in the city and I'd get in the habit of making these mental notes. A railway station or an arcade or somewhere with a spot of green. That'd be a good spot. In case I'm ever a bag lady. I'll remember that spot if ever one day I'm a bag lady. Then I moved in with you and everything looked up again. And of course, now it hits me why you agreed like a flash to move back here. Because you were already seeing him. When we were in Brink Street.

ISOLA: It just feels right, Bea. Children of my own, your nieces—

BEA: Feels right. You looked me in the eye, and lived a lie. That's what I can't get over.

ISOLA: We were going to tell you. When the time was right. Then sort of… slide into things.

BEA: I suppose Carol Donnelly's meant to do the decent thing and slide into a coffin. Then you slide in through the back door. You have to give me your word you're going to break this off.

> ISOLA *turns on her heels.*

What are you doing?

> ISOLA *returns with a suitcase.*

ISOLA: I've been packing things for the past two weeks.

BEA: Open it. I want to see what's in it.

> BEA *opens it.*

ISOLA: You're making things very difficult.

BEA: For once in my life, I'm glad.

ISOLA: If it wasn't for this obsession about Peter Greig and what he's supposed to have done—

BEA: I asked a question—

ISOLA: You ask too many.

BEA: What's moral, what's right—can't have limits. How can you say—this far, no further—?

ISOLA: Other people do.

BEA: This isn't you. He's done this to you. You're not leaving, Issie. You can't. Where can you possibly think you're going?

ISOLA: Get it through your skull, Bea. What would this town be without people like Peter Greig? He opens up people's lives and—

BEA: Opens up lives by giving them a prison. You really don't use your brains.

ISOLA: No. I just fuck. That's all I'm good for. Twice a week for the past five years. Someone who thinks I'm the most beautiful woman in the world. I was a late starter, but I soon got the hang of it.

BEA *picks up a crunched piece of paper, grabs* ISOLA*'s head.* ISOLA *shouts.* BEA *sits her down, shoving a rolled-up ball of paper in her mouth.* ISOLA *spits it out.* BEA *kneels beside her.*

BEA: It's the secrecy keeping this going. Once that burns out the lies will be still be there—look at what he made you do! Lies encase the heart, like oysters growing on top of each other. Hard, calcified.

ISOLA: I need him, Bea.

BEA: Need me! Need me!

Silence. Then a knock on the door.

Come in… It's bound to be a timely letter bomb. I'll open it with my teeth for maximum effect. One way to cure the alopecia.

ISOLA *and* BEA *are surprised to see* IAN *arrive. He takes in the suitcase. And* ISOLA*'s state.*

Well you have to laugh really, don't you? [*To* IAN] I had you picked as an incendiary device. Silly me.

Pause.

IAN: Beatrice.

BEA: Mr Donnelly.

IAN: As I'm sure you realise, people are very concerned about your health…

BEA: Write down the names and I'll send them all a card.

IAN: And in the interests of your health, Council has decided to offer you a termination package. A very generous one. With a glowing reference.

BEA: Probably radioactive.

ISOLA: Bea.

BEA: It's just so hard to tell the knife from the wound.

IAN: Heck, you make things difficult for yourself. If you fight this, you'll never work again. These Yanks don't muck around. It needs your signature by midday tomorrow, or the offer no longer exists.

BEA *is shocked. Then she remembers the ring in her pocket. Not yet beaten, she tosses it in the palm of her hand.*

BEA: The good news is you can ditch the fake. Weren't they right about choir, eh? Such a splendid way to cement a friendship.

She drops the ring in his hand. Pause.

IAN: [*the cases*] Someone off somewhere?

BEA: For a micro-second Issie was thinking of running away.

ISOLA: I am.

BEA: But luckily she remembered you're a coward and a liar—

ISOLA: Shut up.

BEA: If she goes she'll never come back. You'll carry that on your shoulders.

ISOLA: Tell her you're taking me, now.

IAN: Where?

ISOLA: A cave, a ditch. I don't care.

> BEA *reads* IAN, *and begins to leave.*

BEA: [*to* IAN] If you can remember what it feels like—do the decent thing.

> But BEA *reaches the edge of the space, stops and turns. It dawns on* IAN *that she's staying. Slowly he brings his attention back to* ISOLA.

IAN: [*the ring*] Well. I wondered where that was. Christ, Issie.

ISOLA: Maybe it's what we needed. This push. In some ways.

IAN: Carol still gets tired. Very tired.

ISOLA: Maybe because deep down she knows. Maybe if you tell her the truth—

IAN: She's become very wrapped up in Rotary wives. Now that I'm the president. I know that doesn't sound much—God, I don't know what I'm saying—

ISOLA: The push we've needed!

IAN: Sweetheart. The push I need at the moment is out of the Council and into the arms of American Detention Industries. I'll be frank, I've been talking to Peter Greig and—Christ, the opportunities, you can taste them. Then I'd really have something to offer you.

ISOLA: I'll help you.

IAN: Issie, I've met these blokes. They're nice. They're Texans. Run rings around us for manners. At a smorgasbord dinner they stand at their seats until the ladies have all come back to the table and sat down. At smorgasbords. They've got Family Values branded on their buttocks.

ISOLA: We'll be a family. Please help me get away…

IAN: We'll have to talk about this later. Get her to sign—

ISOLA: No. Now. My whole life is here.

She holds his face.

Here. Here.

IAN: [*taking her hands away*] Okay…

ISOLA: Children. That's what you want. I'll have as many as I can.

IAN: I don't know any more, to tell the truth. The idea of bringing kids into a shitty world like this…

ISOLA *is silent.*

Come on. We'll talk later. Hug before I go?

ISOLA, *stunned, allows herself to be hugged. A loud tearing noise as* BEA *tears up the envelope he brought.* IAN *goes.* ISOLA, *in shock, tries to stay upright, but can't. She falls to the floor. Shaking. Stunned. She starts to sob.* BEA *watches* ISOLA *for a moment, kneels down with her, extends a hand and touches her; but* ISOLA *shudders, as if every pore is on fire. She swings herself into a ball, holding herself.*

BEA: We're like two bobbing corks at the moment. Can't take a trick. [*Pause*] Stay there. I'll go and get the hair brush.

ISOLA *moans, too weary to push.*

ISOLA: Get a pillow and hold it over my face. That's what I want you to do.

BEA: Your heart's been broken. That's always hard.

ISOLA: I am trying, so hard, to do the right thing. Trying not to hurt anyone, you included. Who'd think you'd get to thirty-nine and still be waiting… for your life to begin? So bloody weary with waiting.

BEA: Our father used to talk about those trees in the South Pacific somewhere. The explorers would come across them. These white trees. And they'd sail in, getting closer and closer to the rocky shore, because they'd think the tree was moving. Barely a breeze and this tree is shimmering, moving on its own. But really the trees were thick with, covered with, butterflies. And in an instant they'd fly away in a swarm and everyone would be so disappointed because what they'd taken the risk for was a very plain, very ordinary tree. He had no right to lead you on. He'll stay with her, they always do.

ISOLA: No…

BEA: Oh yes. Yes. You're not to see him again. Not in that way. I forbid you. I knew something was going on, I should have asked—

ISOLA: Forbid me. Forbid me? This is all your fault.

BEA: I've never had love from a man, I admit that. Oh, that Jeff chap that time, but not really. But I do understand and—

> ISOLA *pushes her away. She crawls away from* BEA, *making the final, weary break.*

ISOLA: You're a joke, Bea.

BEA: So I will stand by you and be like a rock—

ISOLA: Who wants to live with a rock? Forbid me. You're a joke.

BEA: Tell me you didn't give him all my papers.

> ISOLA *picks up the suitcase.*

ISOLA: I'll call you in a couple of days.

BEA: No. Don't. You won't exist. I won't have to carry you any more. I feel lighter already. I hope you're taking Mother's ratty old clothes. I wouldn't like you to forget that stuff.

ISOLA: No.

BEA: They're in the spare room.

ISOLA: Burn them, I don't care.

> BEA *has gone.* ISOLA *closes the suitcase, and puts on her coat and shoes.* BEA *re-enters, carrying the nightdress. She drapes the nightdress around* ISOLA*'s neck. It slinks around her shoulders.*

BEA: Can't have you leaving without this. [*Pause*] Where do you think you're going to stay?

ISOLA: I want to be happy, not always feeling I'm not good enough.

BEA: I have never ever loved you as much as I do now.

ISOLA: I want to wait for him. In peace.

BEA: Peace can be here. I'll make this peaceful. I'll sort out all the rot—

ISOLA: Next it'll be the monument again. Never mind no one wants it. You don't even try to make people like you. You used to be able to put me in a bath of vinegar, and make me think I was floating in milk. From what I know, our father was a disgrace. You'll end up the same way.

BEA: I think we've been wrong all these years. I think our father was disgraced. There is a very large difference.

> ISOLA *picks up the cases, the nightdress hanging around her neck, and goes.*

If you leave, you are never coming back.

TRANSITION. The sound of the choir. A solo voice sings 'Blow the Wind Southerly'.

BEA *is in the Shaw's shop. She looks exhausted, unkempt.* DICK *looks over his shoulder, watching for* PAM.

BEA: Why did my father shoot himself?

DICK: Your mother must have told you all this.

BEA: No.

DICK: Grief… Twenty-eight children drowning.

BEA: But there's something else. Every day in the past week more and more of that boat's sticking out of the sand. Surely it's caused a memory or two tapping at the glass in your mind.

DICK: I wasn't privy to the ins and outs…

BEA: I couldn't go to the picnic that day, fisherman's children weren't invited.

DICK: Anyone'll tell you.

BEA: Anyone won't. That's for sure.

DICK: They were drunk, they misled your father, let's leave it at that.

BEA: Who?

DICK: Come on, Bea. The Lion's Club chaps who hired him that day.

BEA: Misled him about what?

> *Pause.*

DICK: About how many kids he had on board. He took them at their word.

BEA: Did Brent's father know?

DICK: Your father was relying on him to testify. But the night before the inquest, he caved in.

BEA: Go on.

DICK: He'd been prepared to tell the truth, but that night he warned your father that he couldn't. That he'd been pressured to testify the same as the others: that a freak wave was to blame.

BEA: It was.

    PAM *enters.*

DICK: And now you will have to leave. You caused a lot of trouble last time.

BEA: Please. I'm so tired. Everything's turning on a sixpence.

PAM: Dick.

DICK: You will have to leave. As I said—

BEA: I need to clear my name—the three of us, together… A fifty-year-old woman without a reference—

PAM: Well if you got down off your high horse and—

BEA: Apart from anything else, the insurance money would set you and your bloody daughter up for life. I didn't mean bloody daughter. Not bloody. Sorry. Daughter.

PAM: She is set up for life—assistant matron at the nursing home—

BEA: Out of guilt!

PAM: It doesn't matter! What matters is she's got a future—she'll settle down here, she'll have her babies here, and Dick and I will be able to watch them grow.

DICK: Supply them with their first little uniforms, our grandchildren, winter and summer, up through the sizes, into long pants and class captain badges—

PAM: That's enough, Dick. [*To* BEA] This is not an easy place. You're not the only one's had it tough. Andrew was born the very week that bloody boat sank. So you imagine, if you can, sneaking around with a pram, ashamed of your first taste of joy because half the women in this town had just laid out their children in little coffins.

BEA: The Greig family has stolen from you.

PAM: God stole from us and we don't forgive him either. Now. We want those papers back. And any copies you've made. [*To* DICK] Don't we?

DICK: Oh yes.

BEA: Who gave them to me in the first place? Or arranged for me to get them? Do you think?

Pause.

PAM: No idea.

Pause.

DICK: It was a mistake.

PAM: Dick.

BEA: You are involved. You are. Don't you understand that you've been lied to?

Pause.

PAM: Not if we both agree that we haven't.

BEA *leaves.*

TRANSITION to BRENT*'s office.* BEA *picks up the latest* Chronicle *from his desk and reads.*

BRENT: It's news, Bea. It's sticking up out in the water like Jackie.

BEA: 'For the first time since the *Harmony* went down, she can be seen at low tide… Patrick Samson, itinerant skipper… ' You dare call my father that. 'Shot himself in the head rather than face the shame of an inquest.'

BRENT: It's news. History. News.

BEA: But nothing like the full story. Not by a long shot, is it? [*Pause*] They're using you, Brent, to pierce me with yet another dart. See, your readers'll say—the Samsons have always been cursed. Dangerous. Whatever she says about Peter Greig's bound to be a lie. [*She pulls a page from her pocket*] I'm paying for this. As an advertisement. An open letter to the Minister for Justice for you to publish.

BRENT: [*glancing at it*] It's libellous, Bea.

BEA: All of this has been happening to me. If you don't do it, 'A Current Affair' will.

BRENT: I wish I could.

BEA: You said you were going to help me!

BRENT: This is very typical of people like you—

BEA: Like father, like son—

BRENT: Jesus, Bea! Your fucking father ruined my life, I don't owe you a thing. My father still sits up there blaming himself, muttering on his commode.

BEA: They overloaded the boat, but that's not all, is it?

BRENT: Ancient history, Bea.

BEA: So why come out with this fiction—?

BRENT: What the fuck difference does it make? Everybody knows—

BEA: I don't. Tell me. Oh no. You're too spineless. I can go up to the nursing home of course, catch your father on a good day—

BRENT: Typical of people like you, alienating the very people who are trying to help.

BEA: You made promises in exchange for other people's backbones! Issie knew all right. You jellyfish. She always used to say what pudgy little fingers he's got, Brent Bailey. Not what you'd call a man's hands.

BRENT: What do you mean, used to say?

BEA: She's gone.

BRENT: Where?

BEA: I don't know. I don't know where my sister is. And I wouldn't tell you even if I did.

BRENT: She'll come back.

BEA: Oh, you think she'll come back to *you*. Come back to her senses and realise what she's been missing.

BRENT: I think I was reassuring you.

BEA: Dribbling with excitement when she so much as took a breath. She had you picked all right.

BRENT: Jesus Bea—

BEA: At least I know what to ask him. He always liked me, your father. But you, you're the same as the rest of them. You'll do anything you can, anything at all, not to feel afraid.

BRENT: We can't all be heroes, Beatrice.

TRANSITION. The choir, minus ISOLA, *in rehearsal, is singing 'Blow the Wind Southerly'.*

BEA *enters with posters in her hand. As well as a large glue-pot and paint brush. The singing continues over the following.*

BEA *reads from the poster—'The truth about the* Harmony'—*as she pastes it up.*

BEA: 'When you look at the *Harmony* think on this—'

    IAN*'s voice gets louder.*

'At that picnic the drunken heads of families lied to skipper Patrick Samson about how many kiddies there were on board. And then denied it black and blue. Those men know who they are. That was his mistake, that he believed them.'

    The singing builds. But BEA *rises above them.*

'Now we get to the markers in the channel. My father had been away, the sand in the bar had shifted. And who'd been meant to move those markers? The local police sergeant, he was in charge of marine inspection. At dawn the next day after the accident, when little sandals were still being washed up on the banks, that sergeant went out onto the river. And shifted the markers to where they should have been moved six months before. In plain view, and no one said a word. And now on board, minutes before she went down—'

    The singing continues.

'Patrick Samson realises they're suddenly closer to the bar than he thought, begs the teenage boys to keep the littlies still. Keep the fluid cargo stable. So what do they do: yell 'fairy penguins, starboard'. Non-existent, the fairy penguins. The *Harmony* tilted, broached to on the bar and capsized. Those teenagers who survived, they know who they are. The men who pressured my father not to testify at the inquest, who turned him into a scapegoat because they didn't want to share the blame… '

    Silence. The light on BEA *fades and she leaves.*

TRANSITION. BRENT *follows* IAN *as he crosses to one of the posters and peels it off.* PAM *and* DICK *remain where they are.*

IAN: [*reading*] '…they or their sons still run Dunbar today—the Greigs, Maxwells, Ian Donnelly, Councillor stroke Sergeant Kevin Simons… '

    He scrunches up the poster into a ball and tosses it at BRENT.

She's whacking posters up all over the place. I suppose you printed these up for her.

BRENT: No.

IAN: I reckon you did. I reckon she's stringing you by the balls. Where'd she get all this from?

BRENT: I don't know.

IAN: Maybe she saw you one night sniffing round Issie's window, thinks she's got something over you.

BRENT: No.

IAN: Who'd she find all this out from? Carol saw her this morning. Bea. Reckons she was sort of following her. [*Pause*] My life wouldn't be worth living. Look, I know you know what I'm talking about. [*Pause*] It's time she moved away, Beatrice.

> BRENT *shrugs.*

Do her good. You don't think you could give her a bit of a scare?

BRENT: A scare?

IAN: They're going to start these weekly newsletters. How the prison's proceeding. Big circulation. P.R. Every week for at least the next few years.

BRENT: Who's printing those?

IAN: You haven't still got that shotgun?

> BRENT *has.*

A couple of shots around the house. Cops are away overnight at the footie. Leave it up to you to use your imagination. [*He pulls a card from his pocket*] You could stick this under the door, she'd figure it out.

BRENT: [*reading*] 'Cut-price removals.'

IAN: Up to you. Like I said, use your imagination. Isola always fancied you, you know. Never shut up about you sometimes. Oh yeah. She did. You were just too up-front. Bea wouldn't let you anywhere near her.

Sound of a gunshot. TRANSITION. Sound of wind, water.

BEA *is pulling the figurehead out—trying to lug it, walk it, inch it, drag it. She is making minimal progress. She tries embracing it, and pushing. She stops to draw breath. Another gunshot. Lights on* PAM *and* DICK *on a different part of the space. They listen to the distant sound of the gunshot.*

DICK: Didn't that sound like a gunshot? Over by the river.

PAM: Could be anything. A car backfiring, that'd be it. Or more fireworks. People don't know when to stop.

DICK: Moon's gone.

PAM: Doesn't last long. I'll leave you to turn out the light.

> *They have a last look up at the sky and go to bed. There is another distant gunshot sound.* BRENT *enters wearing a balaclava, carrying a rifle and a torch. He crouches down to reload it.* BEA *is stock-still as he searches the ground with a torch for cartridges. The light of the torch catches the corner of* BEA's *dress. He finds her crouching, terrified, next to the figurehead.*

BEA: [*lying*] Listen. Please. If you keep that... what's the word... on your head... balaclava... I won't know who you are. No idea. You could just go now...

> BRENT *points the rifle at her. A rush of power is going to his brain and he's starting to relish it.*

Please. You say what you want me to do and I'll do it. Just—

BRENT: Fucking shut up. [*Pause*] Crawl.

> *He pokes her with the gun.*

Crawl.

BEA: Oh please—

BRENT: Crawl. Keep your head down. Crawl.

BEA: Just please don't hurt me, please—

BRENT: Crawl.

BEA: What are you going to do to me?

BRENT: The way people feel about you I'll probably get a medal.

BEA: Were you sent to do this—?

BRENT: Or blow your tits off one by one—

BEA: For God's sake, Brent, please.

> *Silence. She said his name.*

If you throw that gun in the river, no one will ever know.

BRENT: She could have loved me, Issie, if it hadn't been for you. If you hadn't interfered. That's the last thing I want you to hear.

> *Beat. By now* BEA *is kneeling.*

BEA: That's not true—

BRENT: Shut the fuck up—

BEA: Ian Donnelly.

BRENT: I know. I've known for years. It was just a matter of waiting it out. Which is what you'd a done if you'd had any brains. Instead of rooting around causing trouble.

BEA: If you're going to do it, just hurry up.

BRENT: Turn around. Turn around!

BEA: No. If you're really going to do this, you can look me in the face—

BRENT: Turn around!

BEA: Because, oh my godfather Brent, if this is what I'm up against, I haven't got any more fight. If this is how fragile—all I had was a pocketful of facts I was bound to report—so if this is how putrid—we say 'cold facts', nothing cold about them. They're pulsing, they're filled with blood—

BRENT: Get ready, Bea—

BEA: If this is what people do when they hear the truth—I am ready! I don't want to be here! There's not a soul on earth who'd miss me.

BRENT: Sit down.

BEA: Come on, Brent, you'd do it to a dog. Have the guts. Or does the cowardice just keep drizzling down through the generations… ?

BRENT: Shut up.

BEA: If he's got Alzheimer's, your father, you've got it worse.

BRENT: You don't talk to me about my—Jesus, Bea, the night your old man topped himself I lost my dad forever—he disappeared into his head, I spent most of my fucking life waiting for him to come back—

BEA: Because he knew he was wrong! Because he knew they all were wrong! It's why—

He pushes her to sit down.

—why they could all do what they did to me—

He yanks her head, and pulls it back.

BRENT: Open your mouth. Open your bloody mouth.

He shoves the shotgun into her mouth. His foot holds the butt on the ground.

Yeah. I'm spineless. Never do anything, me. But you're on top of things, you are. Ever wondered how long your old man sat there? You want this. You're destined. [*He steps back*] I'm going to count to three. Right. One.

She makes a noise, the gun muffling her words.

BEA: Please… [*Now she gets the words out. But in her terror she's starting to laugh*] I can't— [*She gestures—her arms won't reach the trigger*] My arms won't—

BRENT starts to panic. He looks around.

BRENT: I can see that. I can see that. [*He finds a stick, and puts it in the trigger*] I'm not a fool, I can see that. Put your two ugly feet on that. Go on. Put your feet where I've told you.

Thinking that to obey him is probably the best course of action, slowly she does just that. Her feet rest dangerously on the stick, the slightest movement and the gun could fire. BEA is silent. The gun is hurting her mouth.

I'm counting to three, right. Then you'll press down on that stick. One. Still want to do some crowing from the moral high ground? Go on, crow. No time. Two.

DARCY appears carrying an overnight bag. She's been watching from the shadows for some time.

DARCY: You're going to have to do it for her. Why not? What difference does it make? People'll still think she did it.

A terrified look from BEA. BRENT is even more frozen with fear.

Or is this something that's all got a bit out of hand? No one'd blame you for feeling that. I wouldn't. Bea wouldn't. Would you?

BEA makes a 'no' sound. BRENT swings on her.

BRENT: Shut up.

Silence.

DARCY: In anyone's books this is very frightening. This situation we're all in. I mean, if I hadn't come along, maybe you'd have made her go through with this. I really believe you could have.

Noni Hazlehurst (left) as Bea and Celia Ireland as Darcy in the 1998 Sydney Theatre Company production. (Photo: Tracey Schramm)

She takes a few steps towards BEA.

So would it be okay if I take this [*the gun*] out... okay?

BRENT: No.

DARCY: I'll give it to you straight away. Then you can decide what to do. Promise.

BRENT *hesitates, then moves slightly away.* DARCY *takes the gun away from* BEA.

BRENT: Give it [*the shotgun*] here.

Silence. And DARCY *does just that.*

DARCY: You really have scared her. That's the main thing.

BEA: Brent, listen. There's no one I'm going to tell. As if the police believe a word I say.

DARCY: I could get rid of it if you want me to. Take it out into the middle of the channel. You can forget this ever happened. Who's going to believe her?

BRENT: I could a just blown you off the face of the earth.

DARCY: She's very lucky. She knows that. Lucky that you're strong enough to know when it's time to stop.

BRENT: What you've got to remember is... that you're a mad-faced fucking bitch.

After a moment, BRENT *goes.* BEA *starts to cry.*

DARCY: Let's get you up.

She helps BEA *to her feet.*

Better get you back to the house.

BEA: No. I don't want to go up there. [*Realising*] I've wet myself.

DARCY: Well, we can't stay here. Come on.

Disorientated, BEA *follows* DARCY.

TRANSITION. Lighting change. 'O Waly Waly' soars through the night air and stops. The sound of lapping water.

BEA: High tide. The poor old *Harmony* all covered up again. [*Pause*] The second before you arrived you know what I was thinking? That if I could seize the chance, I'd kill him instead. That I could do that.

The second that sat in my mind, you appeared.

DARCY: The town looks tiny.

BEA: From out here, yes. I haven't been out here since I was girl… See that sandy island… over there…

DARCY: Yes.

BEA: I've only ever been there the once and never again. Oh. I'm not one for boats.

DARCY: We're okay. [*Pause*] I passed my test.

BEA: You did. Flying colours.

DARCY: No, no.

BEA: The inquest?

DARCY: Yes. Everyone said that as far as they could see there was nothing I could have done. An accident. [*Pause*] And then today. Another test. I passed Celestial Navigation Stage One.

BEA: We're not going that far, are we?

> DARCY *smiles.* BEA *looks across at the town.*

DARCY: So this'll be my last stay here.

BEA: After all that, I'm surprised you don't turn around tonight and go home. [*Pause*] I failed my test. I don't know…

DARCY: [*noticing a star*] Achernar. It's clearing up. Orion. Rigel of Kent. Sirius. They're the ones of the highest magnitude. Imagine forty days to Capetown, no land in sight… and after forty days to see land. To know you got yourself there.

BEA: He could have done anything to you. You were very brave. You could have just run.

DARCY: You're a good person. There aren't many around.

BEA: [*fighting back tears*] Why would you say that?

DARCY: Because you are.

BEA: I don't feel it.

DARCY: You've just forgotten. [*Pause*] The stars are the stable ones. The planets, my teacher says, the planets are the gypsies of the sky. See up there, Achernar? The very bright star opposite the Southern Cross.

BEA: Yes.

DARCY: We could use that, to start working out where we are. Find it through the sextant, bring the star down to the horizon. Then get the maths right. Remembering your chronometer will be out. Remembering to calculate the error. [*Pause*] You will have to go and report him. And whatever else is going on.

BEA: I thought I knew where to go. I don't.

DARCY: I'll drive you. Wherever you need to go.

BEA: [*giving a smile*] Or I could slip overboard. Float out to sea. But it's not my style, somehow. I thought in there, at one moment, when I saw the hate in his eyes, but… no.

DARCY: In the old days, our teacher was telling us, before chronometers, before they could reckon the longitude, when it was all uncertain… The English Fleet was returning from fighting the French. They'd had twelve days of fog at sea.

BEA: I can relate to that.

DARCY: And the Admiral got all the navigators to put their heads together. But on one of the boats, the night before, a humble sailor had come forward to his captain and warned him that, according to his calculations, they were heading straight for the Scilly Isles.

BEA: [*laughing*] I can certainly relate to that.

DARCY: This sailor had kept a chart of the fleet's location all the way through the passage. But a sailor was forbidden to do this. It was considered subversion. He knew about the punishment but he was so sure he was right he felt he had to speak up.

BEA: What was the punishment?

DARCY: They had him hanged for mutiny there and then. On the spot. The next day, the entire fleet piled up onto the rocks of the Scilly Isles and two thousand men were drowned.

BEA: I see.

DARCY: So did he. Even through the dense fog. Even though the trained navigators couldn't figure it out. He had developed his own way of reckoning.

BEA: It almost looks harmless from out here. Dunbar.

DARCY: I don't think it is.

BEA: No.

DARCY: Want to go a bit further?

BEA: Think we could make it to the island?

DARCY: We can give it a go.

BEA: All right then. [*Pause*] As long as we keep a close eye on the tide.

DARCY: Okay.

BEA: Just to have a look. Then we should probably head back…

Lights fade.

THE END

www.ingramcontent.com/pod-product-compliance
Lightning Source LLC
Chambersburg PA
CBHW041931090426
42744CB00017B/2016